JOURNEY
TO IMPACT

Editions Didier Millet
78 Jalan Hitam Manis
Singapore 278488
www.edmbooks.com

Printed in Singapore by
Markono Print Media Pte Ltd

First published in 2018

Cover photo courtesy of Marsio Juwono

ISBN 978-981-4610-52-0

JOURNEY
TO IMPACT

Bringing hope and change to Indonesia's
youth through social entrepreneurship

VERONICA COLONDAM

To my late mum and dad,
for loving me and raising me to be resilient

To Pieter,
for standing by me

And to my children Phil, Adelle and Joey,
You're the utmost delight of my life, my source of inspiration

With all my love

CONTENTS

PROLOGUE

RAVI ZACHARIAS
Author and speaker

To know Veronica Colondam is to know somebody very special. It has been my privilege to know her for many years and to observe the passion with which she faces every task.

It has been said that you never lighten any load until you feel the pressure of it in your own soul. That is true in all great ventures. There has to be a push from within. Yet, no push from within is compelling enough without significant other components. There needs to be a pull from 'without', an external need that has to be met if the world is to be a better place. And even those two factors are insufficient on their own; doors must be opened to allow inspiring support from others who come alongside to make this dream a reality.

The dream that became YCAB was planted in an extraordinary heart. When the vision was first sensed in her heart, Veronica never imagined how her passion would grow and blossom to meet immediate need. But then it went beyond that, she continued into the future with a prolonged dedication to meet the needs of the underprivileged.

That dedication has changed lives and rescued large numbers of the poor – mostly youths who have dropped out of school, and their mothers as well – with creative and ingenious ways of financing and sustaining their efforts at self-reliance. The financial stability they are able to achieve as a result enables them to support their children's education and career training so that they, in turn, can become productive members of their society. That continuity and spread makes this vision truly a change agent for the neediest in society.

A key aspect of YCAB's entire programme is about giving hope and opportunity to underprivileged youth – by enabling and bringing them from subsistence to sustainable self-sufficiency through education. This book tells the success stories of youths who had no future and hope, but managed to change the course of their lives when love was introduced, when they were given the opportunity to continue their education and gain skills for employment.

YCAB is a mission in incredible progress and the journey from its origin to the present is a story worth tracking. The future is even more promising. This is not just the story of one person or one organisation. From the touching personal accounts of birthing babies, to the agonising devastation of the 2004 tsunami tragedy; from scenes of poverty in Kolkata to receiving United Nations recognition in Vienna, the narrative will draw you in with a tender touch and a deep reach. The reason is that this is a story with immense ripple effect. You will connect with hearts and lives. You will be inspired to learn, imitate and even go beyond. It's a story that pulls together the real life impact of a leader who is ever learning and never gives up. If the world is to withstand all the looming threats and dangers, leadership will be the key.

The examples of the discipline needed, the investments made, the despairing moments and the right choices made to turn the tide, are all instructive and truly inspiring. You will see the heart of great need, and the heart of a leader creating noble impact. The most practical side is how well the author makes connections using analogies and stories from her life, the applications of these truths for life itself. Whether it is a meal enjoyed at a table or a family skiing trip, the writer draws heart, capturing the connection between one's private moments and public calling.

So welcome to a delightful taste up and down the slopes of life, learn to climb even against the wind and to soar high in your calling as you bring light into darkness, hope into despair and a dream of sustainability in a world that often presents nightmares. This book is more than a memoir. It truly captures a journey of creating impact with purpose and noble design. This is a lesson in how to build good memories in simple but effective ways. The story of YCAB tells you the 'why', but also tells you the 'what' and the 'how' of making your calling a reality for the now and a growing dream for the future.

In our times, examples such as Veronica's are needed and her vision is contagious because she tells her story as a person who saw a need and successfully met it with incredible impact. If this book inspires even a small number to act, the effect can be huge. God is the author of life and the ultimate author of dreams such as the ones contained in these pages.

I commend these thoughts for your consideration.

PROLOGUE

FOREWORD

KEMAL MALIK

If there's one person who has been very influential to my success today, it is Bu Veronica Colondam, the founder of YCAB Foundation. I'll always remember Bu Vera's words: in order for a change to happen, you must want it for yourself. Throughout my years as a student in Rumah Belajar and as I was studying in college, Bu Vera continued to be the voice that gave me hope to strive for a better future.

I personally met Bu Veronica Colondam for the first time in 2007 when I was still studying in one of the Rumah Belajar that YCAB operates. I remember that day quite vividly. It was the day I received a scholarship from Tokyo Marine, the insurance company where, after my graduation with an actuarial degree, I have worked for the last seven years. Before that, my knowledge of Bu Vera had mostly come from Google; I had looked her up because I was curious about the founder of YCAB Foundation. My curiosity mostly came from admiration for Bu Vera, someone who is successful, yet has the heart to help school dropouts and the underprivileged.

I wouldn't have gotten to where I am now without YCAB Foundation and Bu Vera. When my dad passed away, I had to quit school and start working. My mum was already old and I didn't have the heart to see her working so hard as the sole breadwinner of the family. So I started to work, doing any job I could find: washing bikes, delivering newspapers, and working as a courier.

I realised that I couldn't continue living just barely getting by, and then I found YCAB. My life has had a completely different outlook since that day. I continued my education at Rumah Belajar and earned a scholarship to attend college. In the future I want to continue my education and obtain a Master's degree, but that has to wait a little as I just got married and my focus right now is my young son. Looking back, I am grateful not only that I am able to be financially independent today, but that I am also in a position to help others. Someday, I aspire to become a social entrepreneur like Bu Vera and run a non-profit to help people, because I think there needs to be more Veronica Colondams in the world.

This book shows Bu Vera's journey to bring about change in Indonesia and beyond. Creating change may take a long time and sometimes be difficult, but it is not impossible. I know this book will inspire others to become extensions of goodness, following in Bu Vera's footsteps. I really believe in the work that Bu Vera does and wish her all the best.

FOREWORD

RORO RISNAWATI

In 2008, when I was still a new student, we held a play at Rumah Belajar and that was my first time meeting Bu Veronica Colondam. My first impression of her was how beautiful she was. And I was surprised to find out how young she was! I recognised her instantly because I had always been curious about her as the founder of YCAB Foundation. Though we didn't get to talk at that time, I really admired her for doing the work that she does with YCAB Foundation. Little did I know that she would be the person who would turn my life around.

When my dad was laid off from his work, our family suffered financially. Though I was doing really well at school, the reality was we didn't even have enough money for my transport going to school and back home. Fortunately, I could continue going to school at Rumah Belajar, a place that I would come to call my second home. The teachers at Rumah Belajar are very attentive and they sincerely care about us, nurturing and teaching us, motivating and encouraging us to study well. Bu Veronica's support and encouragement throughout my studies at Rumah

Belajar meant the world to me. She was the one who encouraged me to apply for a scholarship so I could continue my education until now.

Throughout the difficult times of my life, YCAB Foundation has shone hope on an otherwise hopeless situation. Thanks to the work of Bu Veronica and everyone at YCAB Foundation, I am now able to go to college on scholarship and earn money for my family, helping out with rent and bills.

For my friends and me, YCAB's intervention was the turning point in our lives. We used to struggle to get by, just trying to make ends meet. But now, we are empowered and we have big dreams for our futures. We are confident, hopeful, and we are pursuing our passions and our dreams. I am forever grateful to Bu Veronica and everyone at YCAB Foundation for reaching out to us. I hope for the best for YCAB Foundation and Bu Veronica, and that someday the good work that they do will be able to change the entire world just like they changed my world.

FOREWORD

'The award accelerated everything for YCAB: it helped boost our image in the public eye, especially in the media, something I never thought possible or even dared to dream.'

chapter 1

STIRRED & WOVEN

The light in the hospital room is bright, too bright. But I feel that nothing is able to light up the gloom that has been lingering in my heart. Next to the faintly beeping heart monitor, my mum is lying quietly on the cold hospital bed. She has lost a lot of weight, her hair is thinning, her smile is fading away and she is slipping in and out of consciousness. I sit there silently as I watch her slowly dying.

The early spring of 2001 felt more like a long, dreaded winter. 'The mean survival period of someone with your mum's illness is probably between four to five months,' the oncologist, Dr Karmen Wong, had said to us earlier that year when they discovered a tumour in mum's bile duct. The pathology report that followed the operation showed a terrible prognosis. It was a very rare and aggressive type of cancer and a major operation was needed almost immediately.

My mum had just turned sixty-three the previous December. Before she became ill, she had been very much a housewife. When I was growing up, she was not the type to sit me down and talk about life. Teachable moments would be more apparent when we were watching movies, television series or even the news. 'See what happens when you behave like that?' she would say, referring to one of the characters in the television series. Or, 'Life is interesting, who knows how things will turn out,' making general comments about her impression of the movie's plot. She had subtle, often unconventional, ways of injecting thoughts or wisdom into my mind when I was a young girl. She was very democratic as a mother; she never nagged me to do my homework or study, which made me feel very liberated at home. I was given a lot of freedom growing up – from moving the furniture around the house and deciding where the family should go on holidays next, to what to do during my free time. As all mums do, she established some rules, but they were all reasonable and not at all restrictive. She would, for instance, set a curfew and asked that my friends come in and introduce themselves when they came to pick me up before we went out. She didn't want me, her daughter, to get picked up from the side of the road by strangers.

I grew up as a Christian, but we were never a very religious family. While my mum was a Christian, my dad was a sceptic and very much into the subject of eastern philosophy. Even though my dad did not convert to Christianity until later in life, he respected my mum's beliefs and we went to church as a family at least twice a year, at Easter and Christmas.

One thing I learned from my mum was not to let pressure get to me. When I was facing an exam, for example, she would not tell me to study really hard. Instead, she took me out to relax. We would go grocery shopping or eat out and she would encourage me to ease my mind. I didn't fully understand why she did that until only recently. My only daughter, Adelle, suffered a sports injury that tore her anterior cruciate ligament (ACL). The incident occurred just a few weeks before her final International Baccalaureate (IB) exam. At first, it seemed like a curse, but it turned out to be a blessing in disguise. Due to her injury, Adelle could not study much. She was preoccupied with her new physiotherapy regime and learning how to walk again, while battling her swollen knee. Surprisingly, her grades went up from 40 to a perfect 45. Only two people in Indonesia and 20 people in the world, out of more than 60,000 exam-takers, received that perfect score. At that time, I figured there was a lot of truth in my mum's teaching. I have started to see things differently as a parent now, and I recognise that my mum was wise in her own ways.

But as far back as I can remember, I believed that I was closer to my dad than my mum. My dad was a fun and very personable man. Everybody liked him and loved his company. Travelling with my dad was such a joy. We would go on trips to Bandung on some weekends or during the holidays, during which my dad performed magic tricks and entertained people in restaurants, where we often ended up with free meals. He was amazing. I always thought he was the most wonderful man in the universe. I really enjoyed talking to him, as he was always very intellectually engaging. While my mum was more reserved and less eloquent, my dad always had stories to tell. He would talk to me about everything, from how his days went, to more serious subjects, such as philosophy. Unfortunately, my dad passed away due to a haemorrhage when I was eighteen, and there was not enough time for me to understand what our relationship really meant to me on a deeper level. What remains is the impression of his influence in my life, which has created a lasting imprint on my soul.

When I was younger, Mum and Dad made sure that giving and sharing with others was always part of the culture at home. While we were not rich, my parents almost never said no to people or relatives who came to us for help. I didn't know the details of who asked for help, what their specific needs were, or what situation they were in, but I did know that those who came for help never left empty-handed. The spirit of giving was clearly felt at home, and that shaped me to become who I am today. When I give, I give until it hurts. It would have been a different story if I had grown up in a family with a different view of money, and of how material possessions were valued.

But such is life; there is a balance of give and take. My parents taught me to always be grateful when receiving gifts. No matter how small or insignificant, gifts had to be received with utter gratitude – obviously not for their material value, but for the thought of the giver.

One of the most profound memories I have of growing up is how pleasant Christmas season was. Even today, I can smell my mum's delicious *nastar* (pineapple cookies). While my brothers and I enthusiastically decorated the Christmas tree with wonderful garlands, Heintje – the young European singer who was huge in the 1970s (as big as Justin Bieber is today) – would be singing Christmas songs in the background. I miss those times when life was so simple. They were some of the best moments of my life.

※ ※ ※

My mind stopped wandering as my mum's hands moved weakly. Those were the hands that used to warm my heart with their tender touch. I couldn't recall those hands being so frail, but they were then, withstanding all the treatments she had undergone – beginning with the serious abdomen operation to remove the tumour hiding in her pancreatic tube, followed by radiation and chemotherapy. My eyes felt so heavy and I could feel the tears running down my cheeks. Going through it all, my mum seemed so graceful in bearing the pain. My elder brothers and I took turns to attend to her. There was not a single day that we weren't at her side.

Despite my mum's deteriorating condition, she was still conscious now and then. Even though I was pregnant with my third child, Joey, I was determined to spend that time with my mum. A part of me wanted my mum to hang on, to survive longer, but another part of me hated to see her suffer. I didn't know if I was ready to lose her.

However, life didn't just stop then. Two weeks before Joey's birth, I was doing a television interview for a thirty-minute talk show. It must have been the longest thirty minutes of my life, sitting down uncomfortably on the couch with my big belly protruding, answering question after question asked by the host. I can't remember anymore what I said in the interview and I don't want to see the recording. I must have looked horrible, I felt as big as a whale! Two months prior to the interview, I had received the Fun and Fearless Female Award from *Cosmopolitan* magazine. I was literally fearless, having walked across the stage, heavily pregnant, in my long dress by the designer Napitupulu.

Three months went by, which seemed like forever. And then came the birth pains. Having Joey in the midst of the distress of my mum's illness brought me mixed feelings. My eldest son, Philmon was six at the time, and my daughter Adelle was four. While they hardly remembered Grandma's touch, they could still recall how she used to drop by the house before she got sick, brought them storybooks and played sudoku with them. They got to enjoy the presence of their grandma – bonding and making a short yet meaningful connection with her. But when I gave birth to Joey, I realised that my son would not have the privilege of knowing my mum. There would be no time for him to create cherished memories with her. The pain of loss was mixed in with the joy brought by new life.

Shortly after Joey was born, I began to feel lethargic and unwell. I didn't give it much thought, but decided to have some blood samples taken just in case. To my surprise, when the lab tests came back, I found out that while the normal range of a healthy liver would be around 30-70, my test indicated thousands. Basically, I had a liver infection and was suffering from Hepatitis A. I couldn't believe it; I thought the lab must have made a mistake. I went to see a doctor and he said that I needed to be hospitalised immediately. I insisted that I was fine – only slightly dizzy, and I was going to seek a second opinion. As stubborn as ever, I decided on home care. For that, I had blood taken every couple of days to see if I was getting better, but I was not.

As a precaution, I thought it was a good idea to send Joey away to my mum's house so I would not infect him. I had to stop nursing him and I was quarantined for Joey's sake. Although I knew Joey would not remember any of that time as he was only about six months old, deep down I actually loved the fact that my mum would have more time to spend with Joey.

Two weeks went by and I was so tired of being weak and sick that I flew to Singapore to get further treatment. A doctor there prescribed what I thought was a 'magic pill'. It was just the right medication and I started to feel much better almost instantly. I still remember what it was called: Jetepar. I don't even know if it's still in use now. A week following the treatment, as soon as I was well enough, I went back to the office to work.

At that time, in 2001, Yayasan Cinta Anak Bangsa (YCAB Foundation) was barely two years old. My mum and I had founded YCAB Foundation together in 1999. When we first started, we decided to establish an office at Green Ville, West Jakarta. It was close to where I lived and I was familiar with the neighbourhood, so to me it was a logical choice. The office was quite small, with only four staff members, two of whom

– Elsar and Gilbert – are still a part of the YCAB team even now, eighteen years down the road. My office was comfortable, with a minimalist-themed design featuring colourful walls. We didn't have much art in the office as there was no wall space for it. Luckily, the colourful walls were enough to beautify the surroundings, giving our office some charm.

My mum was my best supporter during the early years of YCAB. Her enthusiasm always showed in the events that YCAB held in its early days. She would come to all the events we held to encourage me and to share the joy with me. Her presence was invaluable. Never once did she criticise me in any way. Instead, she was always supportive and happy to be around everyone who was involved in our many projects. At some gatherings, she would even cook for us. She was a great cook, which was the one thing that I didn't inherit from her. There's plenty of things that I can do that she couldn't, but cooking was one thing at which she excelled, while I struggle.

When people think about my mum, they remember her as a relentless prayer warrior. Though there was the unspoken harsh reality that she was counting her last days, she was very gracious and hopeful through it all. Praying kept her strong despite the turbulent time at the end of her life.

Before I went to Singapore for treatment, my assistant Anita asked me whether I was going to Vienna, Austria. She mentioned that somebody from the embassy had called and urged her to put in an application for my visa. She asked this at least twice and because I was puzzled by the questions, I just kept answering no, I was not going to Austria. One evening, as I was stepping out of the office around six, I heard the fax machine buzzing. It turned out to be an official letter from the United Nations (UN) Office in Vienna. Actually, it was a plane ticket for me to go to Vienna. As it was still lunchtime in Austria, I decided to quickly call the sender for some clarification.

'We would like you to attend an award ceremony for the United Nations' Civil Society Awards in Vienna,' said the nice woman who explained to me what the ticket and letter were all about. Still rather confused about why I needed to be in Vienna, I continued to ask, 'So you would like me to attend the award ceremony? But why?'

'I am sorry I wasn't very clear before. Our Secretary-General has not signed the award winner announcement, so it's not my place to tell you more details about it at this time. But I have to do my job as the external officer and make sure you are here,' the lady explained and then said words that were completely unexpected: 'Your attendance is required because you have won the award.'

When she said that, I thought there was a candid camera somewhere! I thought someone was pulling my leg. That was one powerful statement coming from the UN Office in Vienna. I thought she must have made some kind of mistake, but she hadn't.

Time was short, but luckily the visa application went smoothly, and I found myself flying in a plane across the oceans, arriving in Vienna for the first time in my life. Had my mum been well, I would have taken her with me. Before I left, I had gone to see her for some reassurance. 'This is amazing news and you've done well. Just thank the Lord and enjoy it. There's always a purpose in everything. Find it,' she said profoundly with a smile that I will never forget.

At that time, neither of us knew much about the world of non-profit organisations. We were so naïve; I don't think either of us really understood the implications receiving the award would have for the future of YCAB and, as my mum put it, 'the purpose of it all'.

※ ※ ※

My husband Pieter and I landed safely in Schwechat, about a fifteen-minute car ride from central Vienna, feeling slightly light-headed from the long trip. The air felt a little cold in Vienna and I wished that I had worn more clothes. Thankfully, the sky was clear blue with almost no clouds in sight. Looking at the clear blue sky made me think of my mum and how, even then, she was under the same blue sky that I was looking at. The journey as a social entrepreneur can be a little lonely at times. But by thinking of my mum, I found the strength and resolution to carry on; more ready for what was to come than I ever had been before.

We waited at the airport for about half an hour, but the Indonesian diplomat who was assigned to pick us up had not showed up. I looked around at the busy airport and decided to walk around a little but to no avail. We finally decided to take a taxi to the hotel, which had been booked for us by the UN. While I was queuing for the taxi, I overheard an older man wearing a trench coat talking on the phone in Bahasa. 'I am at the airport. I looked everywhere, but I just can't find Veronica. I didn't see her at all,' he said. I chuckled a little before tapping on his shoulder and saying with a smile, 'I am who you're looking for. I am Veronica.' I remember how he looked at me with a perplexed look on his face, before he finally said, 'Oh, I am sorry, but I didn't expect you to be so young!'

I was only twenty-nine when I received the award. I am the youngest recipient to ever receive the United Nations Vienna Civil Society Award to date. That year, there were four recipients of the award, chosen from more than 120 nominees from all around the world. The first recipient was Saida Benhabyles, who worked in Algeria on human rights, women's rights and with victims of terrorism. She was also nominated for the Nobel Peace Prize in 1996 for her role in the fight against terrorism. The second winner was Athanase Rwamo, who protected children from hunger, exploitation and the effects of drug abuse. Through his initiatives, children were integrated into stable family structures, housed or sheltered and found employment. Lastly, Instituto Mundo Libre, a Peruvian non-government organisation (NGO), helped its nation's street children escape drug abuse.

The award ceremony took place at the Vienna City Hall and was attended by the Austrian Foreign Minister, Benita Ferrero-Waldner, Vienna Mayor Michael Häupl and Pino Arlacchi, the Under-Secretary-General of the UN Office in Vienna.

As I walked into the Senate Chamber at the Vienna City Hall, my eyes were focused on the gorgeous majolica fireplace that faced the entrance to the hall. I found out later that the fireplace had been a present from the Guild of Stove and Fireplace Makers in 1885. The walls in the chamber were covered with green silk damask. The ceiling was richly adorned, featuring fine inlay work with gilded elements. The marble staircase leading to the cocktail venue was intricately designed with renaissance carvings. I was glad that I had dressed up for the occasion in this magnificent place. I was wearing one of my favourite little black dresses paired with my pale green long leather coat and matching green batik shawl.

There was a sense of awe as I walked up the stairs into the venue. Pieter took my hand and looked me in the eyes with an unusual gaze. There was this reserved happiness mixed with a calm, accomplished look. He was as clueless as I was at that time, not realising that we were about to embark on a different kind of life-long journey of learning to do good, and do it better, under the privileged shadow of such an award. We didn't realise then that there was a greater plan behind it all. I felt so small and humbled, yet overjoyed by the entire experience. I could not thank the Lord enough for the honour bestowed upon me. Yet, something within me kept questioning what it all meant, and my mum's words echoed in my mind: what was the real purpose that lay behind all the glory and privilege?

There were around sixty people at the event and a small orchestra was playing classical music beautifully in the background. The solemn ceremony was everything I expected it to be. It was a very straightforward event beginning with a short speech from Under-Secretary-General Pino Arlacchi. He then gave a brief introduction to each award, followed by the presentation of the United Nations Vienna Civil Society Award to each awardee. The award came in two forms: one was a medal with UN logo engraved on it, and the other was a beautifully decorated, handwritten certificate with my name and the name of the award with an official seal and signatures from Mr Arlacchi, and Madame Ferrero-Waldner.

I remember thinking to myself, *This is interesting ... the other awardees are in their sixties and seventies and here I am being recognised with them. They've been doing what they do all their lives to deserve this. But me? I felt like an anomaly there. There's got to be something I've done right, or is this just meant for something else I have yet to understand?* I continued pondering. The whole situation made me incredibly curious about the selection process. I shut my thoughts down. I smiled and posed as the award was handed to me.

After the official award ceremony we were ushered to the reception area. I tried to enjoy myself, but the whole time I was there my mind raced back to my earlier train of thought. I couldn't shake the nagging question of why I was there in the first place. *So why me? For the other awardees, it obviously means a lifetime achievement award. But for me, I've only just begun. What qualifies YCAB Foundation to receive such an honour?* As the questions were running through my mind, someone approached me and introduced himself as Gautam Babar. As if he could read my mind, he explained that he was one of the committee members of the jury and he represented the young voice of the UN.

From him I finally got the answer to the 'why me?' question.

He said that the committee of the jury that year was pretty unusual by the UN's standard. There were more young people on the committee and they specifically wanted to have a young awardee for a change. They believed in investing in the future, and this was one of the ways to help accelerate YCAB's growth, in all aspects: branding, credibility, programme implementation, and exposure.

Interestingly, it seems that the inclusion of young jury committee members has never been repeated. To this day, I still recall that moment as my 'divine intervention number one'.

After the Vienna excitement ran its course, my mind returned to the question of how all this came about. I eventually recalled a visit to YCAB by Mr Sandro Calvani, the new representative of the UN Office for the Asia Pacific region, sometime in early March 2001. This visit to YCAB was the last on his list before flying back to Bangkok that day. His visit was a big deal for us at the time. We didn't even know how he had found out about us. Later on, he told us that he had found a letter from YCAB, written by Mike, one of the guys who used to work with us. The letter was just a simple letter, introducing YCAB and explaining details about what the organisation did. He spent a good two hours at the office chatting with my team and me.

A few weeks later, he sent me a questionnaire to fill in. I thought it was just routine data collection of the organisations he had visited. As it turned out, my responses were used in the application for the award. We were barely two years old as an organisation at that time and I couldn't believe the faith he had in me to submit that application for the United Nations Vienna

Civil Society Award.

Sandro Calvani said one thing during his initial visit to YCAB that I didn't understand until later. He was caught on camera when he said these words: 'YCAB has done amazing work in its infancy. In many years to come, I believe YCAB will lead nations.' Little did we know, his words would prove quite prophetic! I only realised it when we were selected as one of the Top 100 NGOs in the world, first in 2013, ranked #74, and then elevated to rank #63 (2014), #49 (2015), #44 (2017) and #40 (2018). How could he know that? He had such faith in us.

After I came back from Vienna, we held a press conference and people started to take interest in YCAB Foundation. That was our first moment of exposure. Without that award, it would have been harder for YCAB Foundation to attain a certain standing in the non-government organisation world. The award accelerated everything for YCAB: it helped boost our image in the public eye, especially in the media, something I never thought possible or even dared to dream. Thinking back now, everything that had happened kind of worked out altogether for the good. Even for the good that we didn't know yet and couldn't foresee.

※ ※ ※

It's still early in the morning when I decide to clean up mum's room. I can still smell her scent lingering. Everything is still the same, as if she never left. I open the windows to let in some air, and take a deep breath. My eyes are fixed upon a newspaper clipping with a picture of me receiving the award in Vienna attached to her prayer desk. I pause for one brief moment with a heaviness in my chest, a painful joy. I am so glad that she got to share that moment with me. I am thankful that the award was a gift to my mum, to me, and to YCAB.

Mum passed away on 16 February 2002, four days after my thirtieth birthday. She must have used all her strength and waited until I turned thirty before she gave up and surrendered her life. I come across a special birthday card she had bought for me in advance in one of her study drawers and break down in tears. I feel as if I am at the bottom of an abyss of sorrow, knowing that she had been thinking of my birthday all along.

No one had ever told me that grief could feel so brutally cold. It makes me feel so lazy and life seems to move in slow motion, strangely heavy. For the first time, a kind of grief that I had never felt before comes upon me. This time is different; because I know deep down there is something more than just sorrow. My mum's death has left me with a tremendous sense of guilt. The guilt is dormant and subtle; it silently lives between my conscience and heart. I didn't realise this until later that year.

※ ※ ※

'Please stick around, it is only a matter of hours if not minutes, Veronica. I am very sorry, there's nothing more we can do,' the doctor said the morning before my mum passed away. The nurse had left my brothers and I with some final documents to sign. At that point in time, we were ready to let her go, and I signed a do not resuscitate order on behalf of my family. Little did I know at that time that I would have to deal with the impact of that decision years later. Although I knew in my heart of hearts that I had made the right decision, there was a debate in my mind for years after – why did I not do everything I could, everything possible to prolong her life?

As strange as this might sound, I found losing my mum harder than losing my dad. With all the complications that occurred following Dad's demise, I wonder why Mum's death caused a deeper grief. Was it because she lived longer than Dad and I had spent more time with her? Was it because of the strength of the mother–child bond?

I remember the day my dad died, I received a phone call from a university in Vancouver informing me that I was accepted into their art programme. I was silent for a moment and then answered, 'Thank you for telling me that, but I don't know if I can go to school. My dad just passed away this morning.'

It was as if I was given no time to even feel anything, I had to make a big decision soon about whether to enrol in university. What was I going to do about it? Who was going to pay for my education?

I needed time to figure out my life. But there was no time. I had to train myself to numb my heart, to shut down my feelings and use my head from that point on to survive. I never thought setting aside my dream to study abroad could feel this brutally isolating. It was a kind of despair that I had never known; it felt as though the sky was collapsing on me. And upon my two elder brothers. There were times when we weren't sure if they could afford to continue their college education.

Everything became so bleak and grey, but I had to take courage and make a radical decision. I decided to postpone attending college and take a gap year to see how things would unfold. I carefully put away my dream, locked it inside my little box of hope and tossed the key away in the sea of whatever-the-future-may-bring.

I took a diploma programme in communications and public relations, hoping it would land me a job after six months. To me, it was the logical thing to do, but looking back now, it was quite an unusual thing for a nineteen-year-old girl to take on such a huge responsibility. I could have run away from the problem and let my brothers deal with it, but I didn't. I could have been stubborn and left my family to attend college abroad. But at that time I was focused on what I could do for other people, not what they could do for me.

Up until that point, I found comfort in making decisions based on logic, completely excluding my heart from the process. I guess there were times I needed to be seen as a strong woman, and as a result I lost, or forfeited, the ability to connect my head and my heart.

It got to a point where I believed that tears were a sign of weakness. It wasn't until a full week after my dad's demise that I broke down in tears about his passing. It was as though I had been living in a nightmare and it wasn't until then that I realised it was a nightmare from which I would never awaken. My circumstances caught up with me abruptly, leaving no room to breathe. Big decisions were demanded of me, and I was left with no time to feel anything, let alone grieve.

My moment of realisation didn't occur until I attended a grief counselling session one year after my mum's death. 'So what do you miss the most about your mum?' the counsellor asked. I knew exactly what my answer to that question was, yet I took a moment to gather myself before answering: 'Her presence.' Then I asked the counsellor, 'Now you tell me what is stopping me from healing? Why can't I move on? Why can't I let go of her?'

The answer was guilt. I had to deal with the unshared guilt of signing the do not resuscitate papers in her eleventh hour without the presence of my brothers. I needed to make peace with myself that I had done what my mum would have wanted me to do. It should have been what I wanted too, after seeing her in such deep agony during the two days before she departed to be with the Lord.

However, in the counselling sessions that followed, the counsellor also detected something else. There was an imbalance in me. He pointed out that there was a missing connection between my head and my heart. He advised that I must try to be more inclusive of my heart and emotions in life. I needed to pave a new way so that the two could connect. I remember sobbing at the realisation of that impairment in me. I always knew that something was odd in me, but I didn't know exactly what it was until then.

I think the disconnect between my head and heart happened right after my dad's demise, as part of my defence mechanism; I switched into a survival mode. The only way I knew to keep going was to suppress my emotions and trust my mind to deal with life's struggles. I shut my heart down and trained it not to feel anything. Therefore, I would not feel pain or experience any disappointments.

A decade after my dad passed away, I began to crave natural balance, for my heart and my head to reconnect, to become more of a whole human again. For the longest time, I had been solely relying on the connection I made with people on an intellectual level, but it eventually became clear to me that it was time to involve my heart and train it to respond in tandem with my thoughts to balance my perspective.

After that last counselling session, I rejoiced in having finally found out what exactly I needed to work on. I was never the same person after that. One change was I found myself to be weepier, in a good way. I'm glad things happened the way they did, because I learned valuable lessons from the experience. I knew then I was a changed woman.

In his book *The Grand Weaver*, Christian author Ravi Zacharias wrote about a beautiful experience he had. He once visited a small town in India, near the Ganges River, called Varanashi. This place is known for making the best wedding saris in the world. A father and son team make each sari individually. The father is the one who knows the colour combinations and the patterns. He directs his son to move the weaving shuttle back and forth, slowly building the design. The son does not know what the sari will look like, he simply trusts his father and follows his directions. Together they weave the most beautiful saris in the world.

I think that was the best analogy of how little things intertwined to create a great momentum for YCAB and myself at that time. We don't really see the grand design of our life until we actually walk through it and do our part.

What started off as a turbulent year ended with good closure. The loss of my mum after already losing my dad a decade earlier was surely not the best part of it all, but looking back now, there really was a good plan behind everything that happened during the stormy seasons in my life. The experience, the highs and lows of my life, have shaped me to become the person – and a leader to some – that I am today.

'... at some point in life, one will arrive at a need that has to be fulfilled in order for one to be fully self-actualised. A need to give and to share will come.'

THE AUDACITY
OF FAITH

'We will begin our descent in fifteen minutes Ma'am. Would you like to have some more tea before landing?' the stewardess asks. I shake my head, smile, and go back to looking at the picture I have on my phone. It is a picture with my mum, dad and two brothers on the Charles Bridge taken twenty-seven years ago, in the summer of 1988, when Czechoslovakia was still a communist country. It became a republic a year after our visit. At the time, my uncle was the Indonesian ambassador to Czechoslovakia and was based in Prague. My aunt had just had major surgery and my mum wanted to visit her. That was one of the reasons why of all the places in Europe, Prague was our first stop on this family holiday. But I felt that there was something more that had motivated my dad to bring us to Europe. A reason I didn't quite understand then.

That's quite a lavish vacation for our family's standards, I thought to myself. But I was cheerfully shocked when my dad broke the news of our European trip, right after school ended. We had never really travelled that far as a family. Holidays were usually spent somewhere in the region, such as Singapore or Hong Kong, or even domestically in Bali or Bandung. No matter where we went, we were always enthusiastic about going on vacations as a family. It was the time we spent together that really mattered. Holidays were especially memorable because my mum would usually have matching outfits made for the two of us. Conflicting feelings would arise; while it was adorable for the most part, I didn't always like the outfit.

Those good old days are locked in my mind. They have become warmly fonder in my heart as the years and decades have gone by. As a child, I remember our house was always filled with music and silly conversations around the table. At every meal, we would sit down and no one got to take a single bite before everyone was seated. No matter how hungry any of us were, we had to wait for the rest. It felt torturous then, but now I know the value of this routine. It is very hard to uphold this tradition in my own household! My kids always have things to do, or they come home late, missing out on dinner time altogether simply because school is so different now. School days were surely shorter during my school years.

These days, the kids leave home at 6 a.m. and don't come back until around 5 p.m. And if there's a traffic jam, they will ask my permission to eat out at the mall near their school or somewhere along the toll road. Saying grace, however, is one thing I have been able to uphold from my parents' home tradition. Whenever we do get to eat together as a family, this is still the one little thing we do. And we always take turns to give thanks.

I am thankful for these beautiful memories of growing up in my family. If I had to choose one word to describe my childhood it would be 'presence'. My mum was always there to welcome us back from school and was always present for us throughout all the aspects of our lives. My dad tried to be as present as possible, but my mum would always offer her time and presence as her gift to us, her children. Later in my life as a parent, I grew to learn that this sense of presence really is one of the instrumental aspects in a child's development. One thing I know is that my mum's presence gave me a wonderful sense of security. The touch of her lips on our foreheads, the butterfly kisses to wake us up every morning and the sweet relief of her embrace at the end of each day, these were amazing constants in my life. There was so much love, beyond just words. The love was felt so deeply that it is and always will be an anchor for my soul.

Mum's warm embrace and little chats about how my day had gone were integral parts of my daily routine. School days were simple. We left home at around 6.30 a.m. and came home by lunch, then we did our homework. The limited chores we did were enough to train us to be responsible but never too much to burden us. My mum's niece lived with us, and she had been with the family since she was young. It was in 1967 when my big brother, Victor (we call him Kiki), was born, that she came from Gorontalo to help my mum with the new baby. Her name is Regina Rantung, but we call her Zus Rin. 'Zus' in Manadonese means 'sis' for sister. As our older cousin, Zus Rin was like the eldest sister in the family.

Zus Rin was also the one that got us through the difficult time following my dad's demise. She was there to bridge each month; her stable income was the main source of provision for the family in addition to what I earned from my first job. She helped us through until we were done tracing Dad's bank accounts and sorting out his business and assets.

Back to my childhood memories, our days at home were mostly filled with the warmth of love, joy and peace. Of course there were days when things just didn't go well, such as when we had too many school assignments. Of course, there were classic territorial battles with my siblings. I remember fighting over simple things such as choosing which TV channel to watch. Our fights usually ended with one or all of us slamming doors, and tears would wet the floor.

But the times that became truly imprinted on my heart were the days when we had no electricity. It was a terrible thing to experience, especially when we had homework to do or exams the next day. With nothing much else to do, we would often find ourselves singing and dancing in the dim light of the candles that lit up every corner of our house.

Those are some of the fondest memories of my childhood, but those days are so long behind me. Raising my own three children, I wanted to recreate those experiences in my own home. I'm not sure if I have established any childhood routine for my children as it's much more difficult to do in this digital age and we do many things so differently. Things like chatting over WhatsApp can sometimes become more common than face-to-face conversation. There's also this growing need to follow — well, to them the word is 'stalk' — my children in real time on Snapchat and Instagram. And here's my favourite: broadcasting our feelings to each other through Twitter while we sit side-by-side watching TV. The world is changing too rapidly and we are bewitched under its digital spell.

※ ※ ※

I sense the change in air pressure in the cabin and know that shortly the plane will land safely at Václav Havel Airport. My reminiscing about the past suddenly stops and I cannot help but feel exhausted and a little bit jet-lagged. I cannot wait for the night to end, but before I can call it a night and recharge, we stop by Kampa Park – a beautiful French restaurant by the riverbank overlooking the glorious city of Prague. I ask myself why people come to this particular restaurant: is it for the view or for the food? I'm pretty sure our business partner is taking us here for one reason: the view. But we have been told that it is also a Michelin-recommended restaurant, so I guess the food will be good, too. I really couldn't care less about eating, and I'm just a bit worried that with fine dining such as this, the night will drag on longer.

After cheering for the opening aperitif, I am drawn by the exquisite view outside the glass windows surrounding the private area in which we are seated. I excuse myself from the table and walk outside. The cool breeze of the early fall weather freshens up my sleepy mood almost immediately.

Over the long and winding handrail marking the restaurant's territory, I see the whole city of Prague open up before my eyes. It is so beautifully lit up in clusters that even the clouds cannot conceal its shine and splendour. Quickly my eyes scan for the Charles Bridge and I find it at two o'clock from where I stand on the patio. My eyes settle on one of the statues, in front of which my family took a picture together some twenty-nine years ago.

I am just so amazed by what I see. This city has stood the test of time as nothing I see tonight has changed from the city I remember from my first visit. For at least half a century, most of its town centre has looked exactly as it does today. Imagine how affluent this city was before. The glory of Prague's past stands resolute against the ravages of time. Prague was once the capital of all of Europe and this shows in the display of one of Prague's wonders – Prazsky hrad. Until today, Prazsky hrad remains the world's largest castle according to the *Guinness Book of Records*. It dates back to the 9th century and houses various attractions, including St Vitus Cathedral and St George Basilica. The complex sits on the hills overlooking Vltava River.

I can see the gigantic complex clearly from where I stand on the restaurant's patio and I can sense its enormous size even from a distance. It is undeniably huge. I take in the image on the water reflected by the lights mirroring the castle on the hills, and its surrounding buildings kissing the end of the Charles Bridge. The reflections on the water mimic the reality of everything around it, then I remember Matthew 5:14–16 in the New Testament that says:

You are the light of the world. A town built on a hill cannot be hidden. Neither do people light a lamp and put it under a bowl. Instead they put it on its stand, and it gives light to everyone in the house. In the same way, let your light shine before others, that they may see your good deeds and glorify your Father in Heaven.

My thoughts wander to how YCAB has grown. From a little spark, it has slowly but surely become a complex of lights sitting on the hills of social enterprise. Coming to the end of its second decade, YCAB has to some extent stood the test of time – at least, longer than the average survival time of a social enterprise as determined by some experts. That means that somewhere along the way, we have gained people's trust and the acceptance that goes naturally with it. YCAB was never intended to stand like a castle on a hill, but just like a little spark of light. But who knows? Maybe one day it can turn into a town that sits on a hill, which cannot be hidden. As the Bible says, no one lights a lamp to put it under a bowl. It is my responsibility to make sure that YCAB is put on its stand, to give light to everyone in the house.

Some questions flash in my mind: *What is it that YCAB has to offer the world? What is it that we do differently that can add value to the world of social enterprise and, moreover, to its beneficiaries around the world?* These questions are yet to be answered completely, even this many years into my learning journey with YCAB. I'm still growing it and nurturing it. YCAB is my third child, born between Adelle and Joseph, who mostly goes by his nickname, Joey.

Like in the night-time view of Prague I had enjoyed from

my window seat in the plane, the lights are reflected on the water. I ponder about how although the reflection of the lights is captivating, it is only a reflection; the beautiful buildings and castles have stood for a least a century and provide the lights for the ethereal reflections. My attention comes back to the present. What a beautiful sight indeed. I hope one day the light of YCAB will shine before others as a unique thing that YCAB has to offer, something sustainable to create change and to transform the world. Even when we are successful, it won't be to YCAB's own credit, or the founder's for that matter. I am very aware that we are all but mere instruments.

The glory is neither YCAB's nor mine, but the One who inspires me to continue my work. The formula is simple: God loves me, I love the world. God's love is bountiful and it has a spillover effect. The spillover effect of that love is my responsibility to share His love with the world.

Take YCAB's name as an example of my intention: *Yayasan* means 'foundation', *Cinta* means 'love' and *Anak Bangsa* means 'the children of the nation'. So, YCAB's name means 'Love the Nation's Children Foundation'. Just like Prague's buildings and castle stand with their beautiful reflections on the water, my hope is that one day, YCAB can stand on its own solid ground and continue to reflect God's love to those in need.

'Madam, it's time to take the food order. The gentlemen are waiting inside,' the waiter says, breaking my reverie. He takes my hand and guides me down the steps of the patio. I smile at him while trying to conceal my excitement at the connections my thoughts have made between YCAB and the lights in this memorable city of Prague.

Seven gentlemen including my husband are waiting at the table to order our meal. They look fine while welcoming me back to the table with smiles on their faces. I see they are enjoying a few drinks. Bottles of red and white wine have been selected and poured. *That's good, the waiting wasn't that painful,* I think to myself and unconsciously smirk. But then I catch a glimpse of a couple of men at the end of the table who look very sleepy, and I feel a little bit guilty that I got lost in my thoughts outside.

For some reason, the sight of the men waiting at the table for me reminds me of the summer camp that my mum sent me to when I was twelve. I was always late to the dining table and everyone had to be seated before we could say grace and begin eating. During that five-day camp, they almost always had to wait for me.

The camp was indeed one of the defining moments of my life. It was there where I realised that I delighted in trying to understand and compare world religions in general. At that summer camp – it was actually a Bible camp – we were given the opportunity to learn about other world religions such as Islam, Buddhism and Hinduism, and their concepts of God. We also explored the absence of God in atheism. We did this to better understand what Miroslav Volf of the Yale Divinity School called 'sufficient similarities', and causes of tension between beliefs.

In the subsequent years after camp, I found that I enjoyed engaging in discussions with friends from different religious groups and learning about their beliefs and various points of view. Understanding the tension between religions – even amongst denominations inside one religion – was the most intriguing part of the conversation. For me, every conversation about faith matters. I always find it fascinating that one can believe in something one doesn't fully understand. Through conversation, we can easily tell whether a person adopts a belief for real reasons or out of convenience. I personally think a person must stand for something that they truly choose to believe in and that 'what they believe in their heart must make sense in their mind', the same motto as that of one ministry that I care for. If the heart and mind are in agreement, it will bring a sense of peace and profound joy.

In my case, I have become more and more inclined towards Christianity since that time of my life. Its truth really sank into me, not just at the level of my heart, but on an intellectual level as well. The depravity of man in his sinful nature is hopeless, and the sovereignty of God will provide a Way to salvation. For the first time, my mother's faith made sense to me.

The story of my father's faith, however, was a different case altogether. I remember him as a sceptic, albeit a sceptic who was very respectful of my mum's faith. He went to church at least twice a year, on Easter and Christmas. I remember that was a big deal to my mum; it brought a big smile to her face. She would prepare herself all day, pick her prettiest dress and drag us kids and Dad to church. We all knew that Dad usually falls asleep during the service, but that didn't stop Mum from being joyful.

Although a doubter, Dad was still sincere in his search for *something* in which to believe. This desire led him to read books by the world's greatest thinkers on philosophy, especially eastern philosophy. It was because of these readings, I'm sure, that he began to meditate every night. I guess it was important to him to meditate on everything that he had learned, and try to synchronise it in his heart and mind. Maybe his meditation was simply a state of calmness that he needed to finish his day. I didn't really think about it, as I was a young girl then. I don't even remember when he started his meditation routine. All I know is that he used to meditate every night until long after everyone was asleep.

Every night things went pretty much the same at our house. We said our goodnights to Mum and Dad and we hugged, then the lights were turned out. But one night, something happened that was completely different from any other night. It was like a Narnia moment, where an hour on earth was equivalent to years on the other side. I think that was what my dad experienced. And when he told us about his experience, we couldn't believe our ears.

'The entire room was dark and I was sitting lotus-style on the floor,' he told us one day. 'In all the tranquillity of the night, the only noise I could hear was your mum's breathing deep in her sleep,' he continued. 'I fell into a trance. I think I had a vision.' His eyes were dimmed. 'What vision, Pa?' My two brothers and I asked curiously, almost simultaneously.

Trying to remember the details of his experience, he cautiously continued, 'There was this uncontrollable notion that moved my right hand. My arm was extended straight into the air, my index finger pointed into the air, and it began drawing three crosses in a blazing fire.'

He paused a little, trying to steady his breathing. Then he said, 'When I saw those three crosses before my eyes, I heard a voice calling me by my childhood nickname. "Toan, it is I whom you seek. I have come to find you. Though your sins are as red as crimson, they will be as white as snow." Suddenly I felt convicted of all the wrongs I've done in my life. Then I began to sob.'

There was a pin-drop silence amongst those of us who had gathered around him. Since we didn't really know what to ask, we decided to wait for him to continue. 'Then the voice asked me to find the book that Mum often reads: the Bible. I was led to some readings. Knowing that I wouldn't know the names of the books of the Bible, the voice directed me to open it at specific pages, so that I could read particular verses. Page after page I was brought to my new knowledge. As if the voice knew about my previous struggle with atheism, I was shown in a simple narration and all my doubts just vanished!' His eyes were on fire as he continued, 'Then I was guided to see God's inescapable plan to redeem us all. It just came to my understanding that no one can save his own life by doing good, simply because human standards of good fall way below God's standard – they are never on par! It is only through God's grace that salvation is provided. The only way we can be saved.'

Listening to Dad talk about his experience, I thought to myself, *This is what I was taught at Bible camp. I'm very sure that Dad has heard those sentences many times before in all the church services he has attended. But none of it ever connected to his heart and mind when he was always buried down in his slumber or lost in his own philosophy.* Then I smiled a little as I thought:

It really took a special divine visitation to bring all those words to life, to have meaning. This time they just made sense to Dad.

Dad told us that his spiritual encounter felt as though it went on for a very long time. By the time he came out of his trance, all the blazing fire was gone. He found himself back in the dark room still sitting in his original position. But there was this one thing he couldn't explain: he now held the Bible in his hand. When he glanced at the clock he saw that it was almost dawn. He woke my mum up and whispered, 'Beth, I want to be baptised.'

Between the obvious surprise and her drowsiness, Mum thought she hadn't heard Dad correctly. But looking at his serious face as he repeated his statement, she felt a deep sense of joy and fulfilment. *No time to lose*, Mum told us she had thought to herself. *Better arrange everything before he changes his mind.* Within just a few hours of dawn, Mum had come up with a solid plan for this glorious event – something for which she had been hoping for almost twenty-three years, since they got married. On the following Sunday, 2 June 1985, my dad was baptised on a beautiful summer morning.

Many a time I have looked back on Dad's story, his extraordinary spiritual encounter, and wondered if it actually happened the way he said it did. It is not easy for anyone to believe or just accept that God Himself really came to speak to my dad that night. What was so special about him? Why Dad? Not only was he taught about the narration of God's love to each individual that leads Him to provide the way to salvation, but Dad had mentioned that they were also engaged in some kind of debate. They wrestled with my dad's past philosophies, all the readings that had shaped his thinking and understanding, pretty much everything to which he had been exposed. I didn't and I still don't know exactly what their conversation was like, but I recall Dad saying this in conclusion of his encounter: 'Everything became as clear as crystal. Everything makes perfect sense now. All those books of philosophy that I read, each of them actually carried a little glimpse of God's truth. I feel at peace now. Everything is tied up beautifully. The puzzle in my head is stacked in order. It just clicked!'

What a bizarre experience to have had as a young teenager. I was merely thirteen when all that happened. However, looking at the drastic change it made to Dad's life, I can only believe that it was truly God's work. In the days following Dad's experience, he began to speak differently. There was a new authority in his tone when he ministered to family and friends.

He also said that he was compelled to pray for people. He even laid his hands on the sick – some terminally ill – and they were healed. I can name each of them who are still alive today. They all shared with us the same detail: that my dad's hands became burning hot during the prayer. In some cases, they reported the feeling of an electric rush going through their bodies, and then feeling 'lighter' or 'better' immediately. When they would go for a medical check the next day, they received a clean bill of health. Some were even miraculously cured of cancer.

Something else that was special was Dad's sermons. He would quote word for word at least a thousand verses without any mistake in one speaking session. Yes, we did count the number of verses he used, each with its exact chapter and verse. It was as if he were weaving many verses together and they became strands of perfect sentences, which were then woven into a powerful message.

It was beyond my comprehension that anyone could ever do that. We were all amazed by his newly acquired skills. It was a very powerful thing to witness right after his 'Narnia moment'. Had I not borne witness to all that my dad experienced and his life after his spiritual encounter, I wouldn't have the strong courage to tell the world. I figure that my dad's spiritual experience is also valid as a spiritual experience of my own – and, of course, for everyone in my family, too.

This brings me to a unique position of faith. My mum inherited her faith from her family, and Dad found his through a personal supernatural encounter. Having witnessed first-hand these two extremes, I have become very open to anything that comes in between, or even beyond. I will not be quick in passing judgment on any dogma or denomination. I will not dismiss any personal encounter that people claim to have had with God in whatever way they experienced it. I simply will not. It is because I have seen proof from both camps – as far apart as the north from the south, or the west from the east – this reality really brings me home, home to my own experience.

Dad's ministry really intensified in the years that followed his awakening. Sometimes I wonder if Dad knew his time was limited and because of this he stretched his savings to take the whole family to Europe. It was like his way of saying goodbye. Three or four years into his ministry, he suddenly had a stroke and died five days later, on Good Friday of 1991. We buried him on that Easter morning. He was only fifty-one years old.

❉ ❉ ❉

The chef comes to thank us for allowing him to cook for us that night, and my mind quickly snaps back from my thoughts of the past. Everyone seems happy with the dinner and thanks the chef kindly in return. Checking whether we have some space for sweets, the chef offers us some of his special desserts of the day. I see everyone shaking their heads in response; we are all either too full or too tired to enjoy dessert, and we regretfully decline the offer. The stony street leading back to our hotel is not friendly to my heels. After struggling on the fifteen-minute walk, I am so ready to depart into slumber land.

❉ ❉ ❉

'Mum, I got seven on all of my assignments and quizzes. But I didn't get a seven as my final grade,' Joey says to me, rather despondent.

'How's your relationship with your teacher?' I ask him.

'What do you mean?' he asks with a puzzled look on his face.

'Has your teacher ever complained about your behaviour? Have you been found non-submissive to his or her requests?'

He goes quiet for a moment, looks slightly embarrassed, and then says, 'Well, I guess. Sometimes.' Continuing the conversation, I later advise him to fix his relationship with his teacher, because that's what life is all about. We can't rely solely on our intelligence, and life is not just about facts and data. It is about finding connections with people, and a lot of the time we need to connect with people who have authority over us. 'You have to find that connection, and make that connection with your teacher,' I say to Joey with a smile, ending our meaningful conversation for the day.

One thing that I have learned from the school of life is that there's a limit to intelligence. When intelligence can't take us any further, it's time to give way to something smarter than mere intelligence. To me, it's called a relationship. When IQ stops, EQ (emotional intelligence) takes over. And EQ can take us the extra mile we need. Being able to build relationships – especially befriending our foes – and trusting our hearts can open many doors.

When I think about IQ and EQ, I am reminded of what Steve Jobs – arguably a highly intelligent man – had to say about the value and importance of following your intuition. He said the following in his speech at Stanford University's commencement ceremony in 2005 (quotes from this speech went viral following his grim prognosis that year):

No one wants to die. Even people who want to go to heaven don't want to die to get there. And yet, death is the destination we all share. No one has ever escaped it and that is how it should be, because death is very likely the single best invention of life. It's life's change agent. It clears out the old to make way for the new.

Your time is limited so don't be trapped by dogma – which is living with the results of other people's thinking. Don't let

the noise of others' opinions drown out your own inner voice.
And most important, have the courage to follow your heart and
intuition. They somehow already know what you truly want to
become. Everything else is secondary.

※ ※ ※

When I celebrated my twenty-sixth birthday I had a strange
feeling, something akin to a grim prognosis in my soul. I, too,
was face to face with death. Not a physical death, but it almost
felt like a spiritual death. I'm not talking about denying my faith
or losing my spiritual anchor or anything, it was actually *because*
of my faith that I was faced with the true reality of emptiness.
The desolation within me occurred because until then, I was not
living my life to the fullest. I was living it for myself.

Death – or the feeling of it – is the *single best invention of*
life. It's life's change agent. It did change me. It brought me to
a place where I needed to make priorities in my life. My first
priority was to fulfil a vacant spot in my life. As the Hierarchy of
Needs goes, I think that what Abraham Maslow's theory argues
is actually true, that at some point in life, one will arrive at a
need that has to be fulfilled in order for one to be fully self-
actualised. A need to give and to share will come.

If I remember it correctly, everything was fine. In fact, my
life then was more than 'alright'. I thought I had it all, a good
husband and two wonderful kids. All my needs were relatively
well taken care of. Yet, there was this tremendous feeling of
emptiness deep inside of me. I felt there was something missing

from my life; something that I needed to do; something more than fulfilling my role as a wife and mother; something that would give more meaning and purpose to my existence. I was restless, not at peace with myself and I knew I was in search of something greater.

As people gathered at our place for my birthday party, and as the pastor talked about the significance of life and what success meant, I found myself trapped in a web of the multiple tracks in my mind. 'Success isn't what you think you have achieved. Success isn't something you arrive at when you are still alive. It is when you die, when you're inside your casket. What people remember about you determines whether or not your life was a success.' As soon as I heard the word 'die', it threw me into an imaginary dialogue with God. I imagined I was dead and God asked me what I had done during the life that He had given me. I searched for the right words with which to answer Him but was too stunned to respond. I could have said, 'Well God, I've been busy with my life: dealing with my dad's demise, going to school, doing some work, getting married, and raising a family.' But I shook my head, negating my own defence.

Then I started to imagine my tombstone. I wondered what would be written on it.

Veronica Colondam

A wife. A mother.

And what else?

I kept hitting a wall. I thought I needed another word to describe my existence besides 'wife' and 'mother'. There's nothing wrong with being just a wife and a mother, but in my case, I needed to fill in the blank of that 'what else'. But why did the 'what else' mean so much to me? Why did those words keep haunting me? Why couldn't I just be satisfied with being a mother and a wife? All these questions continued to build up until I came to my single contemplation question: How do I want to be remembered?

As I thought back on those questions, I was reminded of a parable I read many years ago. It's about a king who was leaving his kingdom for a time. Before he left he called his three servants and gave each of them a number of talents. The first servant was given one talent; the second, two talents; and the third, five talents. When the king came back, he wanted each servant to be accountable for the number of talents he had given him or her. The king wanted not only the principal talents to be returned, he expected interest.

The servant who was given five talents was able to gain five more. The servant who was given two talents also doubled his talents like the other servant. The king was pleased with these two servants and called them good and faithful servants and invited them into the king's glory. However, the last servant who had only been given one talent said that, out of fear, he had hidden his talent so he could at least return the principal to the king. The king was outraged with this servant and his reasoning.

※ ※ ※

'Make a wish and blow out your candles,' Pieter whispered gently in my ear. My gathered family and friends were waiting for me to perform this tradition. His voice snapped me out of the jungle of my thoughts. *Oh wow, the fellowship is over,* I thought to myself. My mind must have been so preoccupied that I didn't even remember which song we sang at the closing of the fellowship. Then the guests started to approach me to congratulate me, and we bid our goodnights and goodbyes.

The birthday celebrations finished when everyone left that evening. But my imaginary dialogue with God remained. It actually stayed stronger deep inside as it demanded more out of me. It demanded real action. 'Action' was the one word stuck in my mind.

There are many people who seem religious but are actually devoid of good deeds. They enjoy the worship, but don't take any real action to share God's love with the world. They remind me of the conclusion of the story of the sheep and the goats, otherwise known as The Judgment of Nations from Matthew's Gospel. At the end of the day what distinguishes those who will inherit the kingdom and those who are cursed with eternal fire, is what they were willing to do for a stranger in need.

'Then the righteous will answer him, saying, "Lord, when did we see you hungry, and feed you; or thirsty, and give you a drink? When did we see you as a stranger, and take you in; or naked, and clothe you? When did we see you sick, or in prison, and come to you?" The King will answer them, "Most certainly I tell you, because you did it to one of the least of these my brothers, you did it to me."'

I think the underlining theme of this parable is that what we're doing for the least of the people around us, we are doing for

God. So there should be real action that goes hand in hand with faith. That was a powerful realisation that really spoke to me.

Something else spoke to me, something my dad used to say with a certain look on his face. A look I always felt was directed solely at me. I didn't know whether he meant it that way, but that's how I remember it. It didn't mean anything much before, but it was brought into a different light at that point in time. He said, 'Of those to whom much is given, much is required.' But given what? Then I realised he was talking about a vast range of gifts in life: talent, capacity, capability, unique experiences and so on.

For some strange reason, I began to be reminded of how unique my experiences were growing up. Looking back, I remembered throughout my school years the two things that came naturally to me were leadership and fundraising. I found it quite odd that even in a new class where all my classmates were pretty much strangers to me, I was always appointed as the class chief or the treasurer or secretary – I still don't really know why or how. I found it to be pretty bothersome because I had to do extra work to organise things for the class.

Speaking of extra work, during my service on the student council, I was led to do even more extra work. Regardless of which title I held on the council, I was always trusted to do pretty much the same thing: to raise funds. Then, because I was involved in a lot of fundraising activities, I would miss a lot of school days and have to retake some of the exams and quizzes.

Because of this, I also learned about managing school politics, at the simplest level, and tried to convince my teachers to let me retake some of the exams that I had missed. Or, on some other occasions, I had to negotiate with my homeroom teacher to adjust my absent days. Otherwise I would have failed the class because I had missed more than twenty-eight days in a single semester. I had to think hard about how to win my teacher's heart. After all, I missed all those days because I was working hard to make money for the school events they had asked me to organise. No teachers ever helped me. I did all the work with my classmates, from pitching the idea of an event and standing before the sponsorship committee of the prospective companies, to closing the deal – or being rejected, which occurred multiple times.

The only way to waltz my way out of it was to win my teachers' hearts and to make the 'connection' that I would later teach Joey about. I would find out my teachers' birthdays or work anniversaries, which then gave me reasons to give them extra attention. In some cases, I would even do some investigative work and find out what the teachers needed and raise funds from my classmates to find the perfect gifts for them.

Besides serving at school, I also learned a lot from serving at church as a pianist. I took part in the music ministry at church for a long time, until I gave birth to my first son, Phil. People say musical training helps the brain and improves mathematical sense. I have personally never experienced any proof that those particular theories are true, but my years of serving really gave me more confidence and flexibility. This responsibility also gave me clear focus. I had to practise and always be prepared before each church service when I served as pianist.

Later I found that the training I had of playing in front of hundreds of people for years really helped me with my confidence. Being in a different church band later taught me about delegating tasks to my team. On both occasions, improvisation was key. And I learnt that delegation comes with risks.

Once a task is delegated, we must give authority to others to make decisions in our absence. Hence there is risk. But it trained me to think of the worst-case scenario and to think about how I would deal with it if it happened. I was always prepared with the best possible way around potential problems. This, I believe, was my first encounter with leadership.

Now looking back, I realise that my unique set of experiences and skills developed in my school years and at church had been my training, as if I had been running a mini YCAB. I learned skills by doing, and also from my mistakes. It was the infancy of my development as a leader.

I can't believe I have been fundraising all my life – starting on a small scale at school to now, on a global scale. All I know is that I just kept completing the tasks at hand and delivered, though when I was working on those tasks I didn't always see the bigger picture. But I learned that when we are faithful in doing small things, bigger things are waiting.

From my small journey of belief, to the more supernatural exposure of my dad's conversion, I landed at my own crossroads as I turned twenty-six. My life took an exciting turn when I renewed my life's mission and refocused on my calling. All the skills I had learned as a child helped me become the person who I am today. It all converged and brought together the three parables that have repeated in my heart and head since. The parable of the sheep and the goats, the parable of the talents, and the parable of salt and light were put into perspective.

As for the parable of salt and light, light is very profound – what you do is made visible and apparent because of light, but we are not the source of the light itself. The source of light must be something greater than us and, in my understanding, it is God. And then, there's also salt that dissolves and flavours the food, which I think has something to do with popularity, fame, and the spotlight that goes hand in hand with the element of humility.

Just like salt, my presence needs to be felt, but I need not be seen. Salt is also used to preserve food; that's how the perpetuity thinking came along: to preserve the good things YCAB has done. YCAB's mission and cause have to remain long after I am gone.

The feeling that there was something I must do with my talents and my unique experiences grew stronger. More than anything, I felt it was demanded of me. This feeling led me and reassured me about my calling over the eighteen months following my birthday. I needed to work everything out so that when my king came, I would be found a 'good and faithful servant'. I would be held accountable for all the talents entrusted to me and I would return as many additional talents as possible.

There was no time to lose. Finally, on 13 August 1999 my mum and I founded YCAB Foundation and signed the incorporation papers. It was, at last, legal. All of my desire to do something good for the world was neatly institutionalised.

So the three words that kept me going were: talent, action and legacy. What was next, however, still remained unclear.

'People want painless processes, instant results and successful lives. There's nothing wrong with that, but it doesn't happen very often.'

3

PAIN AND PLEASURE

I awake to the gentle kick of baby Adelle in my stomach and a heavy and deep contraction in my back. I glance at the alarm clock on my bedside table – it's around four in the morning, and the sky is still pitch black behind the curtain in my bedroom. Trying to gain full consciousness, I struggle, walking slowly towards my bathroom, tiptoeing carefully so as to not wake Pieter. *It's about time*, I think to myself. Carefully, I shower thinking *I need to wash my hair*. It will be days before I get the chance again. Under the hot water running down from the showerhead, I pray to God that He will give me the strength to deliver my second baby today.

The contraction intervals shorten, and the pain that is so familiar to me starts to kick in. Even though it is still relatively mild, I know that it is the beginning of welcoming our baby princess into this world. 'Pieter, wake up. We need to get to the hospital. Why don't you shower quickly while I get ready?' I shake my husband out of his slumber, whispering those words into his ear. I remember it is a holiday morning for the Ascension Day of Christ. 'Do we have everything we need? Have I forgotten anything, you think?' Pieter asks me while dragging out the small roll-away luggage that I had prepared for the hospital. 'I think we've got everything there. If we forget anything, we can just get it later. You can always come back, it's not far,' I say with a smile, containing the pain and trying to stay as calm as possible. Because of the early hour and the fact that it is a holiday, the roads are clear of traffic and it takes us less than fifteen minutes to arrive at the hospital.

The stinging fresh smell of antiseptic mixed with medicines washes over me as soon as I walk through the hospital doors. 'Coming through, please make way, this lady is in labour,' I hear the nurse who admitted me into the hospital say as we make our way to the delivery ward. I am alone in the ward as Pieter is busy dealing with hospital registration. Before we had gone our separate ways, I told him to call my mum and to ask my brother to drive her here.

Minutes later, a senior nurse comes to help me change into a hospital gown and examine me. I can't help but feel a little nervous, thinking about the unbearable pain that is to come, like that I had experienced with Phil, my first child. 'You are dilated to four centimetres, so we're looking at several more hours to half a day. Until then, please try to be as calm and as relaxed as you can be and think happy thoughts,' the nurse says with a soft-spoken manner and smile on her face. *Evidently she has been doing this for years, of course she is calm. For her it is a job. But this is a matter of life and death. I wonder if she can give me the number of women in labour who are able to be 'calm and relaxed'. And did she really just say 'think happy thoughts'? Who could have happy thoughts in between contractions of unbearable pain that keep on escalating? I would be lucky if I had any thoughts at all!* Before I lose myself completely in my grumbling inner monologue, the nurse continues, 'The doctor will be here soon.' With that statement my train of thought is broken.

In hindsight I realise that for the births of all three of my children, I started to have my contractions around four to four thirty in the morning. Each of my three children was born on either weekends or holidays. Interestingly enough, for each labour I arrived at the hospital at almost the same time, around six or six thirty in the morning. It was as if it were planned beforehand, so that Pieter would always be there to take me to hospital.

As the nurse closes the curtain behind her, my mind races back to the time when I was about to give birth to my first child, Philmon. I was a rookie then, but the length of my pregnancy wasn't as long as the doctor thought it would be. At that time my own gynaecologist, Dr Yani Toehgiono, was still on his summer holiday. Phil was impatient to leave my womb and he did so two weeks earlier than the doctor's predicted due date. Dr Yani's colleague had come in to attend to me. He was also a senior gynaecologist but he wasn't convinced at that time I was feeling the contractions as painfully as I should have been.

※ ※ ※

'So, between one and ten, what is your level of pain?' the doctor asked. I was silent for a little bit, trying to access my brain's hard drive of pain, and connect it to what my whole body was experiencing. It was my first childbirth. I didn't know how to rate this pain, as I had no baseline to begin with. Without an experience of other pain to compare it with, would my answer be justified? *Will the doctor grasp the intensity of my labour pain if I say a number in response to his level-of-pain question? The threshold of pain is subjective to each individual. Will my answer correlate to the pain that most women feel at this stage in labour? Will it be the 'right' answer? Is my 'five' the same as other women's 'five'? More importantly, is it the same as the doctor's 'five'?* All these questions roared through my mind. But I guess, in the end, pain is pain.

So I answered the doctor hesitantly, 'Perhaps three or four?' Unsure, I was just guessing the numbers. Then I watched for the doctor's response. His face was blank. *Did I answer correctly? Was it consistent with the rest of his exam?* Somehow I picked up a signal that the doctor was unconvinced. After he was done writing on my chart, he looked straight at me and asked, 'Your pain is at a three or four ... but you can still read a book?'

Oh no! I had given him the wrong numbers. They must be inconsistent. I thought to myself. From the look on the doctor's face, I knew something wasn't going the way it was supposed to. After a short discussion with the nurse who stood beside him, the doctor continued, 'I don't think the opening of your cervix, the interval of your contractions and your level of pain are consistent. You are dilated to more than four centimetres, with less than fifteen minutes between contractions.' He paused a little allowing me some time to fully understand what he was saying. Then he continued, 'People don't read a book at this level of pain. We better induce you.' *Induce me? What is that? Gosh, did I miss reading about induction in the book that had accompanied me throughout my first pregnancy* (What To Expect When You're Expecting)? *Why didn't they say anything about induction? What does it mean?* The doctor's blank expression scared me. I felt like I was being sentenced after giving a wrong answer on a final exam. I didn't even care if he thought I was ignorant, I gathered my nerve and asked him 'What's an induction, Doc? What does it do?' His answer was light, 'Oh, we need to bring you to a level of pain consistent with your contraction intervals and dilation. Don't worry.' His 'don't worry' actually made me even more worried! Why would he say 'don't worry' if induction didn't usually make people worry? Without waiting to see if I had any questions or concerns, he quickly ducked behind the curtain while telling the nurse to prepare for an induction.

I was still puzzled when the doctor left. I felt like he made all the decisions about my labour and I hadn't even been included in the process. Then I heard a curtain at my right side slide open. There was a weak yet firm voice saying to me, 'Sorry, but I overheard what the doctor said to you. You know, you can say no to that.' The woman in the bed next to mine paused as a contraction came. 'Induction means the pain will be so much stronger then it normally would be. And trust me, it's already painful enough!' She cringed as if remembering a strong pain. Then she said, 'This is my fourth child, so I know. Believe me, you don't want to be induced. Tell the doctor you want a natural birth.' *Wow, I thought this was a 'natural' birth that I was anticipating. What's more natural than this? What does she mean by 'natural'? Isn't this as natural as it can get, labour without C-section?*

Then she continued to mutter, pausing occasionally, waiting for her contractions to subside, telling me about the differences of pain in all of her four deliveries. Trying to convince me that with an induction, the pain would be worse than normal. *But really, what is 'normal'?* I pondered. *This is my first time, I won't know the difference.* The more she talked, the more threatened I felt. This was not what I needed. Too much information could lessen my courage to deliver for the first time. *Let me be! Let me experience this myself!* I screamed silently beneath the mask of my polite face. I thought to myself, *I better stop her.* So I thanked her for her kind warning and then, as though she knew I couldn't take any more advice, the nurse came back in and began making preparations to drip the so-called induction into my veins.

Approximately half an hour into the induction, the pain escalated to a point where it was almost unbearable. *The lady in the next bed was right. I should've listened to her. I could've said no.* The contractions came more frequently and the pain was more intense. It was probably the most intense twenty minutes of my life. The intensity stimulated me to push, so I kept pushing as the pain came crashing over me. In the midst of all that, I somehow heard the senior nurse say in quite a panicked tone to the other nurse, 'Get the doctor now, the head is close!' I wasn't even thinking, let alone worrying about how to deliver the baby without my doctor's presence. The pain almost overcame me. I felt like I was drowning, trying to stay afloat and gasping for air. I was in so much pain that all I knew was to push, so I kept pushing hard. Minutes later, the doctor arrived and he quickly sat down on his stool and the baby came out. The baby popped out of me, and was caught by the doctor just in time!

The moment that followed was a moment of tranquillity, of peacefulness; it felt as if I had accomplished a mission: a mission to bring a baby into this world. In that split second, I heard the high-pitched cry of my baby Phil, born weighing 3.33 kilograms and fifty centimetres long. All the pain was gone. It had been replaced with a bliss of joy and satisfaction. *I've made it. I am someone's mum now.*

Only those who have already gone through labour, both with and without induction, can know the difference. I was naïve and ignorant and I didn't know any better during Phil's birth.

It was just like when I birthed YCAB. I didn't know how to run a non-profit, let alone understand how and what to do to create change. Obviously the pain of running an organisation was one thing, but the pain of not knowing what to do to create change or impact was the harder reality to handle.

In the same way induction expedited my labour process, all the hurt and pain we experienced when we 'birthed' YCAB helped us to accomplish our goal at a rapid speed. Later in YCAB's journey, we were 'induced' by our lack of systematic approaches to improve how we operated. We needed to put in place a process for patching up a situation and controlling whatever damage had been done. For example, lacking a procurement system could lead to employees stealing from the company. If that happened, it wouldn't be 100 per cent the employee's fault. While they were faced with a choice and chose to do the wrong thing, the organisation, which did not invest in a good procurement system, would also be at fault for exposing people to temptation. In short, it is our responsibility to put in place a good system for our organisation to operate on, and both internal and external inductions are needed for an organisation to grow at a faster pace and be better. This is especially true in the non-profit business. We need to do good and do it well, as we are under more scrutiny than for-profit organisations. Only good organisational systems can create systematic change. This 'system' covers a broad spectrum of issues from governance to impact, from managing talent to creating a conducive ecosystem, including policy making.

The way labour is approached has changed so much over time. Nowadays, out of fear of pain, many mothers-to-be choose to have an epidural during labour. I don't understand that as I think pain is a mother's most valuable sparring partner during childbirth. You need to feel the intensity of the pain to push, and finally give birth to something beautiful. If there's no pain, and we depend on a machine to monitor the need to the push, the push power won't be as raw and powerful as it should be. But what do I know? Times have changed and comfort is the name of the game now.

People want painless processes, instant results and successful lives. There's nothing wrong with that, but it doesn't happen very often. In labour, we have the choice of an epidural, but in life what is our epidural? What is the one injection that we can have to ease all the pain? I wish there was one! At the organisation level, anything instant is desirable but in my experience from growing YCAB, instant achievement may lead to unsustainable results. Painless process is good, but not necessarily great.

※ ※ ※

'Dr Yani is here but he's in the other delivery room with a lady who is having a long and difficult labour. But yours won't be difficult, I'm sure. Your first child was delivered quickly, right?' I nod while my racing mind remembers that fateful induction day, the voice in my head saying, *Of course it was fast! The induction did it all!*

As I ponder those words, I have a strange awakening. There is a sense of pleasure in my second labour pains. When you have been exposed to a worse kind of pain, the pain you are currently experiencing can feel lighter. Strangely enough, it can almost feel pleasurable. That's exactly how I compare the two births. The pain that induction brought was terrible. If I could rate it now, it was a twenty out of ten! But the horrible induction of Phil's birth really made my experience giving birth to Adelle like a walk in the park. Adelle was born at 9.25 in the morning on Thursday, 8 May 1997, two hours after the first examination by the nurse and Dr Yani. She weighed 3.26 kilograms and the memory of bringing her into this world is locked in my mind. It was what a labour was supposed to be in its most 'natural' way. Now I know the difference!

Adelle's birth was beautiful and graceful, unlike Phil's birth, which was quite brutal. With very little time between contractions, I felt like I was drowning. What the lady in the next bed told me that day was so true. I could and should have refused the induction, but I guess I was exposed to the two different labour experiences, two different kinds of pain, for a reason. At the very least, I can say now that I've done it both ways. Tragically, after two 'normal' births, I finally know what 'natural' birth is like. Normal doesn't always mean natural. That was a new lesson for me.

Growing YCAB was almost like a combination of Phil and Adelle's births. The first half-decade was brutal and filled with headaches. We were still unclear about a lot of things, as all we had back then was the courage to want to create change in the world. But since none of us – neither founders nor management – came from a non-profit or impact space, an 'induction' was needed to really take us out of our comfort zone so that we could learn more about how to do good for others well.

The first induction we experienced involved funding and programme content. In terms of funding, because we didn't know any better, my family underwrote all costs. Up to a certain programme size, we realised how unsustainable this was since our business units were still unable to support YCAB, as they were yet to make a profit. The escalating pain was felt at the programme level, too, when we faced difficulties with schools.

We thought bringing free youth programmes such as soft-skills training was going to be accepted everywhere. Little did we know that without certain incentives, schools weren't so keen. It was very complicated as all these incentives were costly. Some schools expected us to provide food, some demanded to be paid per student who attended our programme. That reality of the situation completely perplexed me. It was shocking and utterly disappointing.

Considering the early difficulties we had, the second half of our first decade was relatively easier. We understood how things worked a bit better. On the funding side, we celebrated and welcomed our first multinational programme partner, Unilever. We leveraged on this first association to work with many more corporate partners in later years. These developments gave us more negotiating power with the schools. And on the programme side, the induction of YCAB's first five years was more into the pain of tracking our data and measuring impact. That, however, was carried forward to the second decade. Now as we are in the second half of the second decade, we are experiencing another induction, which requires major organisational restructuring and serious change in management. Believe it or not, we are still experiencing this sort of brutal induction, even with all the experience we have gained.

Yes, there is different pain at every step, but overall the organisational pain keeps escalating in proportion with our ambition. Experts say that scaling is a normal progression in any organisation's life cycle or curve. Contrary to my birthing experience, organisational inductions come and go naturally in order for the organisation to fall under a normal curve.

Within our induction periods, we found our 'epidural' here and there, the kind of joy and painless state that reminds us why we do what we do. Those people, the ones who support and encourage us, are like the epidural in our veins.

On a personal level and as life went on, I was exposed to more opportunities to expand my threshold of pain by being exposed to different kinds of pain. I have now built my very own spectrum of pain, and I can place each pain experience on that spectrum. It's very useful as a baseline.

Labour pain comes and then goes away. It comes at the right moment to drive you to push a new life into the world. It is a temporary pain after which you get an amazing reward wrapped in a huge bundle of joy. As soon as you hold your baby in your arms, all the pain dissipates. But what about pain that doesn't go away?

There are other kinds of pain that stay with you for as long as you live. I have one. It is a physical pain I have had to accept and live with since I was sixteen or seventeen – a back injury that I suffered during my training as a badminton player. I was left with two herniated discs between the L3 and L5 vertebrae of my spine. By now, those discs are dead. To a layman's eyes, the discs have become dark and look as though they have melted into the spinal bone when seen in an MRI scan. It sounds terrible, but there are worse things that could happen, such as if the discs were undead. 'Undead' means that the disc can still slip in and out of place, which could lead it to protrude and pinch the nerves around it.

One can only understand this crippling pain if they have experienced it first-hand. There was one episode that I endured during which I could neither stand nor sit and I had to lie down on a hard plank mattress for days while recovering. There was this deep and sharp pain going through my back, brushing through my outer thigh and down to my toes, and when my body moved in a certain way, I felt like I was being electrocuted. I had to wear a tight back brace to make it more bearable – not gone, but bearable.

There were days when the pain escalated and became excruciating to the point that painkillers became my best friend. I was well aware that painkillers don't actually heal anything, they just trick your brain into not feeling the pain. Yet the pain remained, because the injury was not dealt with. Despite all that pain, I still thanked God that when those discs died, they died within their own space, which meant there were no pinched nerves and the discs weren't protruding. If they did not, I could have been left in a state of persistent and more severe pain. I came to conclude that less pain is better, and I could only know that because I had experienced both. One thing this condition brought me was a constant, yet bearable, soreness on my outer right thigh. It's the kind of pain that, from time to time, wakes me up in the middle of the night. When this happens my other best friend is always at my bedside, and its name is Hisamitsu's hot patch.

The key insight that I gained and found very interesting was that I wouldn't have been able to appreciate the comparatively walk-in-the-park birth of Adelle had I not experienced the ferocious induction of Phil. The two experiences were needed in life to come to an understanding of the spectrum of pain. Without pain we wouldn't be able to deeply appreciate pleasure when it comes. As C.S. Lewis rightly puts it in his book *A Grief Observed*, pain amplifies pleasure. Pain is simply needed to understand and appreciate pleasure. If pleasure is all we experience in life, how can we know that those pleasures are pleasures, let alone pleasurable? We would be numb to those pleasures. And when pleasure has lost its purpose, isn't that the most tragic thing, more tragic than pain itself?

In his book *Where Is God When It Hurts?* Philip Yancey explains that the state of painlessness isn't always the best thing. He writes about people whose damaged nerves have cost them the ability to feel pain. As a result, they may cause themselves serious bodily harm, losing fingers or other body parts. Sometimes they don't act to prevent themselves from such injuries simply because they can't feel the pain.

One example he mentions in the book is about a little girl born with leprosy who kept biting her fingers until they were so damaged, they had to be cut off. She did it because she thought it was a fun thing to do. He also tells of a woman who accidentally put her hands on a hot stove and didn't realise that she had badly burnt her hand while preparing food for her family. Healthy nerve pain would prevent these things from happening. Healthy nerve pain can prevent us from seriously hurting ourselves as it makes us react to painful stimuli. Sometimes when we feel pain it is a good thing, because it gives us the signal to stop the activity that is hurting us. For example, had they been able to experience pain, the young girl would never have bitten her fingers, and the woman would have removed her hand from the stove before the burn was too severe.

Organisationally speaking, if there is no pain in growing the work we do, then we need to be careful lest we become complacent. The absence of pain can be a symptom of organisational leprosy. Organisational leprosy is the one factor that can handicap a good organisation and prevent it from becoming great.

Pain and pleasure therefore must exist in life to balance our existence – not only to balance, but to put our existence into a more meaningful perspective; meaningful because we can tell that the absence of pain is called pleasure. And when pleasure arrives, we can recognise it and celebrate it. Since my first labour experience, less pain for me was already a pleasure! And at the end of the day, I realise that pain and pleasure both have to occur in life to make things beautiful. The timing factor can be outside our control as well, unless we actively make an effort to create a system to organise our life, or our organisation, to fulfil its purpose of existence.

I learned that painful experiences refine me. Like having a sparring partner to motivate me to score better and fight harder, I appreciate induced pain as a wake-up call about a problem we may have. Painlessness is also not always a good thing. I became more convinced of this after being injured during a skiing holiday.

※ ※ ※

My accident happened in 2007 during a family vacation at Thredbo ski village, just a two-hour drive from Canberra, Australia. Much like my three children, I grew up being athletic. Skiing was one of the sports we all enjoyed, and we were all having fun until my fall. I was skiing downhill when I fell while trying to avoid some trees. While I continued to roll downhill I felt something pop in my knee. A few skiers came to help me up but I thought I was fine. After a few minutes the pain subsided and I began to wonder what I should do. *Should I walk up to the chairlift? Or should I try and ski down?* I didn't feel the latter was a good idea. So I decided to walk up and found an attendant at the chairlift station.

'I fell down and something popped in my knee, and I'm not sure if I should ski to the bottom of the slope. Can I take the chairlift?' I asked. The attendant took a careful look at me and then answered, 'No, our regulations won't let you take the chairlift down. Let me call the ski ambulance for you.' I was a little surprised by her reply, and I answered while shaking my head, 'No, no, no, I've just had a minor fall, and I can still walk and all. I don't think it's anything serious. I don't think a ski ambulance is necessary, really.' I moved my body in a certain way while explaining this to her, and for some strange reason I lost control of my legs and fell again. *Oh gosh, what's happening to me? Why did I fall uncontrollably like that?* As if she knew what was going on in my head, the attendant said while helping me get up, 'I think your knee gave way.' *What 'gave way'? What does that mean? Is it bad?* Before I became more anxious, she continued, 'Plus, it is our standard procedure here. No matter their condition, every injured skier has to be taken down by ski ambulance.'

She sat me down on a little bench just outside her post while saying, 'Wait here, let me make the call.' *Boy, look what I have gotten myself into. They're just overreacting, I don't need a ski ambulance! That sounds way too serious for such a minor fall. My knee doesn't even hurt. Besides, I hate to create a scene being taken down by ski ambulance. A million skiers will be watching me – such an embarrassment that will be. Not to mention how this will scare Pieter and the kids.* I was contemplating all these thoughts when minutes later two guys arrived. They helped me to the ski ambulance and strapped me to an orange stretcher. *Now it's official! Great, everyone will see this. An orange stretcher stands out against the white snow. Gosh, is this really necessary?*

Another lady with a red cross emblem on her bright yellow ski jacket asked me a bunch of questions about my family, who to call and where to reach them. In a flash, they skied me down the slope on the orange stretcher, and a loud siren accompanied us all the way down until we reached the healthcare facility. I could only imagine the countless pairs of eyes from the hundreds of skiers who watched me as they had to make way for the ski ambulance to pass.

When we arrived at the clinic, Pieter was already there. From the look on his face I could tell he really thought something seriously bad had happened. From the way they had strapped my forehead and my chest to the stretcher, it looked like I had at least broken my neck or something. It looked really awful. 'Don't worry, it's nowhere near as bad as it looks,' I said with a smile on my face, trying to convince him that I was okay. 'I fell and I can still walk. But they wouldn't let me down on the chairlift. This was the only way down,' I said as I was lifted on to the clinic bed. I could even sit up a little in the bed and when he saw this, Pieter started to believe that I was actually alright. I told him my knee was painful for a few minutes after the fall. But there was no pain afterward.

While I was telling him the story of how I fell, I could hear another patient being wheeled in. Separated by a thin, see-through curtain, I could hear a young male voice screaming to the max. I stopped my conversation and tried to take a peek. I saw an Australian teenager being injected with something, and in a count of about ten seconds, the boy calmed down. *Ah, it must be a morphine shot. I think that kid broke his leg or something. A bone fracture is super painful. I don't feel any pain so I should be okay. I don't actually understand why I am here.* Honestly, I was still confused as to why my falling down had caused such a commotion.

'What do we have here?' a friendly voice asked. The smiling face of the doctor on duty became visible as he pulled the curtain aside. He asked me a few questions and I explained for the umpteenth time what had happened and how I fell. I kept making jokes that I wasn't in pain like the kid next door, that I should be fine. But after he examined my leg, the look on his face made me worried. 'I think you lost your knee ligament.' He demonstrated what he was saying by bending my knee. 'You feel no pain because it's a complete loss, not a tear. The only way for you to have the stability to walk again or do sports is through surgery.'

I was completely shocked. I couldn't believe what I just heard. 'If it were torn, you'd be in pain, like the kid next door,' he added with a smile. 'But his case is much worse, it's a total fracture. Nasty injury!' As if I would feel better with that comparison. I just couldn't accept that my painless injury needed surgery. The doctor instructed the nurse to measure my leg and put me in a knee brace. From that point on during our holiday, a knee brace accessorised my leg.

From that ski village we continued our journey to the Gold Coast in Queensland. There I met with a knee surgeon, Dr Vertullo, who was the colleague of the doctor at Thredbo. He told me, 'Why don't you go back to Jakarta, as I can only do the surgery eight to ten weeks from now, after your knee has healed. In the meantime, elevate your leg and compress your knee with ice packs five to six hours a day.' *Gosh, this will be a drastic lifestyle change! How can I ice my knee for six hours a day? How can I work this way?*

Ten weeks later, I found myself travelling back to Australia to repair my anterior cruciate ligament (ACL). The surgery was successful, and I was as good as new in four to six weeks after the surgery and therapy. However, the pain of the surgery and rehabilitation left a kind of trauma in me. Four months after the surgery I was as good as new, but the scar remained. I didn't think I could ski ever again after enduring the pain of recovery. The pain was actually more of a mental pain or trauma. The fall and the surgery were fine, they weren't that painful. But the pain of having to discipline myself with daily rehabilitation exercises, including physiotherapy for six months following the surgery, was a different kind of pain that I never wanted to experience again, even though I knew that the rehabilitation phase was necessary to make sure my knee was completely healed. In the end, my leg healed and was stable enough for me to wear my heels again. During my recovery that was one of my greatest motivations and ambitions!

Any orthopaedic surgeon will tell you that the success of a surgery is dependent on timing. My surgery was a success because I waited for the swelling to go down before going ahead with the invasive procedure. It is also wise for organisations to wait when they are faced with a wicked problem.

As YCAB's leader, I've learned not to be reactive but proactive, to be cool headed and emotionally unaffected before diving deep into a problem. For example, I took time to decide YCAB's new structure. A few years went by, but I wasn't comfortable making any big decisions until the right people with the right skills and capabilities appeared. We couldn't have changed the structure if I was still uncomfortable with the team. With Mario Montino and Stella Tambunan to serve alongside me – as YCAB's new group COO and CFO respectively – I finally found my peace.

From one pain to another kind of pain, I have learned that both are necessary. Like in life in general, we leap from pain to pain, only to learn that the entire spectrum of pain is necessary to appreciate life as it is. Painful situations are meant to bring the best out of you, not to tear you down.

There is no such thing as a painless or suffering-free life. I also learned that painlessness doesn't always mean that there is no injury or trauma; on the contrary, it could mean total devastation, even worse than a painful situation when pain is felt. Painlessness can actually be numbness. If we feel no pain, we should search deeply. Is it because there is no trauma or is it just that we can't feel it?

In my experience of pain, I also learned that there are different kinds of pain: physical and mental pain. Mental pain tends to linger far longer and deeper than physical pain. Take my ski injury – my injured knee is now better and stronger, but I still don't have the guts to ski again. The other important thing is the lesson in feeling the pain. I really think one needs a 'pain sparring partner', not just to match the pain, but to help give birth to something new and beautiful once the pain is endured. Like labour pain, only when pain is escalated to a certain degree are we are able to enhance our strength to push us to a limit to innovate, to give birth to something fresh and new.

A pain sparring partner in life sometimes refers to the wicked problems and terrible situations we face. As they escalate, so must our strength to endure and our hope for deliverance. Because of this I feel as though I've become a stronger and more understanding person who, at this point in my life, can confidently say that I am unafraid to embrace suffering. Not that I go looking for it, but it is best to face it head on when it comes rather than try to avoid it. One will probably learn much more by working through the difficult situation, to understand what suffering is like, to really feel that we have defeated pain and suffering and what it feels to live beyond pain. Simply put, suffering brings out hope, and hope is good for our soul, especially hope for deliverance. Hope is what keeps us alive, keeps us striving, enduring and innovating. Therein lies the beauty of it.

Organisationally speaking, the philosophy of pain is pretty similarly applied. Painlessness does not always mean everything is good; instead, it can mean the worst. Just like with my ACL injury, a lack of pain actually means surgery/action is necessary. In running a business or growing an organisation, we must be on our guard when we feel that there is a lack of pressure or problems; this situation may lead to complacency. For me, complacency is the greatest enemy of growth and therefore success. We need to continue to ask ourselves, is there truly an absence of pain in the organisation because it is run so well? Or, is it the management team or the organisation leader who is not aware of the organisation's problems? Many times a leader can be delusional in thinking he or she is already doing great, leaving little room for improvement.

In some cases, however, and this is based on my experience at YCAB, wicked organisational pain will remain dormant until it reaches its peak point and one day it will blow up, surprising everyone. When that happens, it really can cripple the organisation. Almost like the 'organisational leprosy' I noted before, the lack of pain sensation does not mean there is no pain or no danger of crippling our body parts. On an organisational level, there are times when a problem is so dormant that if we do not address it quickly, it can ruin a division at best, or the entire organisation itself at worst.

YCAB learned this the hard way. For the longest time we did

not have a human resources (HR) manager. Yes, even though we had grown from four to 700 employees in sixteen years, we simply thought a payroll officer would do the trick. But we were all busy with so many things growing YCAB, expanding its programmes and businesses, that the HR function was overlooked. We had talked about it a lot, and we understood the need, but we never really focused on putting together an HR team. Until one day when a senior officer reported to me that there had been some movement to petition the management team. This movement was intense and involved many employees who had signed up to put pressure on management.

That made us realise that, yes, all our employees were here to serve, but who served them? Well, I want to believe there's one big draw to working for a non-profit: in addition to decent monthly pay, it docs bring a certain value of meaning and purpose that for-profit companies cannot compete with. But this isn't the case entirely. Even though non-profit workers are called to serve, they should still be part of a system where everyone feels that they are cared for. They need to feel that we empower them and develop their skills. Most importantly, they need to feel secure about their future, for example, when they retire. There should be an HR programme for this. However, such programmes require a budget. We had the intention, but no one took the final step of running the numbers so they could be approved. Years went by and this had not made it to the top of our list of priorities. We needed someone to do the serious planning and projection.

Thankfully, YCAB is a social enterprise. That means we

generate income ourselves from the businesses that we have, which gives us the liberty to allocate funds for employees' welfare and to implement an HR programme. Imagine if we were a purely charity-driven organisation; it would be so much harder. At our current size, we need to have enough financial cushion to put aside a budget for employee benefits and a pension plan. This situation was really the reason we held our first ever town-hall meeting, making more effort to communicate our HR plans in order to fix this organisational pain. This is one of the examples that created a situation with organisational 'mental pain' for me. It provoked a kind of leadership trauma.

I am now grateful for the pain that my crew at YCAB has had to endure under my watch. They have been more than gracious about waiting and working things out together as a team. The lesson here is to never overlook the people. Raising funds is not easy, but it is harder to find good people whose hearts are set for social-enterprise work. Now we have an HR team and HR issues are being dealt with one day at a time.

Since then, I have continued asking myself, what's the mental pain this year? I cannot let it keep scarring YCAB from the inside; anything hurting from the inside really needs more serious handling. I know at each turn, in each phase, there will always be issues and pain that I need to be aware of. It is only in a culture of continued conscious awareness that we can find problems, resolve them, learn from them and move on.

Birthing YCAB was one thing, nurturing it is another. From an induced labour pain to an understanding that mild pain is already a pleasure, I am no longer afraid of pain. All the little pains make life more memorable. The proof is that as life goes on, we tend to remember traumas more vividly than all the normal things we go through. And what is 'normal' doesn't always mean natural.

Organisationally speaking, just like my induced labour birthing Phil, induction is needed to force us out and bring us to a new phase. In YCAB's case, it snapped us into making a very serious effort to resolve our human resources issues.

As much as induction is sometimes necessary and inevitable, it actually shouldn't be avoided because through it we learn so much, we discover our true selves when we respond to the urgent need at hand. Like giving birth without an epidural, I take every problem YCAB has as its sparring partner that will help it to grow and to fight harder. What better sparring partner for pain is there than the pain itself?

I make myself very mindful of any painless state as it can lead to organisational leprosy, in other words, complacency. Complacency usually requires organisational surgery or, in some cases, an amputation just like the restructuring we're going through that requires us to let go of people who are unfit for their roles. Mindfulness could have prevented this. That, I believe, is the best thing for an organisation, and life itself.

'I trembled because of the paradox I saw: I saw contentment in them, and gratefulness. They had almost nothing, yet they maintained their dignity.'

chapter 4

CATALYTIC MOMENTS

An email that came through one morning made me think. Not because of its content, but because of the intimidated feeling that I immediately felt in my stomach when I read it. It was an invitation to speak at the Asian Development Bank's Inclusive Business Forum. The invitation came from someone I truly respect, someone who had shown deep interest and care for YCAB over the years. His name is Ron Perkinson. Despite my many doubts, I decided to do it, knowing that Ron would be there to moderate the session.

It was late February 2016 when I found myself in Manila, the Philippines. Entering the building, I could feel a sense of anxiety within me. After stopping at the security checkpoint to get my ID card for the week, I walked through the cold halls trying to remember where I was supposed to meet Ron.

The lobby looked pretty bare, with just a few black leather sofas; suddenly I wondered whether I was on the right side of the building. The building was massive, and in such a building it is easy to become disoriented and lost.

Just as I was getting worried, I received a text from Ron; he said he was coming to get me. A few minutes went by and we finally met. Ron walked me through the agenda and then he told me that there had been a last-minute change and he would no longer moderate the session, but would be a panellist like me instead. I was even more intimidated. But I braced myself, not sure whether my face showed that I was only pretending to be brave. I tried to remain calm although I felt so unsettled inside. I prayed that the new moderator would be kind to me as I found myself shaking his hand when Ron introduced us minutes later.

The following day was the presentation day. The idea was for me to present the uniqueness of YCAB's education programme, which is tied in with access to capital for the mothers of the students. That is one of the key features that create sustainability, which everyone loves. As like in many presentations, I began by showing YCAB's logo as it speaks about its premise of change.

'As you can see, at the base of our logo there is an icon that looks like a book – not a bird,' I quickly scanned the room to see whether my audience realised that the icon really looked like a bird. Usually some of them do and it makes them smile. Some did this time, too. Then I continued, 'And that represents education. As long as we invest in it wholeheartedly – as you can see with the heart symbol there – education will help create better welfare.' I paused for a second, then continued, 'And welfare is represented by an icon that looks like a house. Believe me, it is not an arrow, it's a house.' When I said that, I saw wide grins on many faces in the audience. I loved to know that the audience was with me, that I was connecting with them. The bottom line is, our logo represents everything YCAB stands for. It reflects our premise of change, that education is the basis to create better welfare.

With the next slide, I explained YCAB's three pillars: healthy lifestyle promotion (HeLP); education, called HoLD (house of learning and development, also known as Rumah Belajar in Indonesian); and HOpE which stands for hands-on operation on entrepreneurship and/or employment.

'With these three pillars, what YCAB has created is a holistic development programme through which we try to improve the overall Human Development Index of Indonesia,' I made that emphasis to close my presentation on the particular slide. 'Do you know how I came to this perspective?' I saw some faces show more interest. Then I said, 'Every time I use the words "youth development", there's one name that comes immediately to mind: Pak Ferry. I can't help to think exactly when I became aware of what really we do at YCAB, which is now widely known as "youth development". This perspective was brought to light by someone who was practically a stranger to me at the time, but who later became a friend.'

I thought it would be good to share with the audience how the term 'youth development' came about. I was invited to a talk at a popular online community gathering, held in the garage of an old house somewhere in the centre of Jakarta. They brought in speakers to broadcast live on Twitter and other social media. At that time, YCAB had already established all three pillars – HeLP, HoLD, and HOpE – but we hadn't really found an overarching word to represent what we were actually trying to achieve as a whole. That night I was paired up with the Dean of BINUS Business School. I had never actually met him in person before, but I had heard of him, and everybody called him 'Pak Ferry'.

Just before we went live, Pak Ferry and I were talking about what we did, and about YCAB. Something came to light, something that never crossed my mind. Pak Ferry looked at me intently as I explained at length what YCAB was all about. He nodded here and there. Then he put things into a new perspective, when he asked me, 'Are you familiar with HDI, the Human Development Index?' I quickly responded, 'Yes, I am.' Then he continued to say, 'Do you realise that YCAB has naturally grown to cover the exact three pillars of the Human Development Index? What you are doing is actually a holistic development programme, Vera.'

It was such an eye-opening moment for me. Now all that we do made more sense than ever before! Ever since that night, I knew that we had earned the right to use the term 'youth development' as YCAB's overarching theme. We had earned it in the space of health, education and economic empowerment.

I just couldn't fathom the grand scheme I was playing a role in; it was like I was at the mercy of God's guiding grace and He sent random people to light up my way from time to time just when I needed them. I find it to be one of life's beautiful surprises, when people give me fresh perspective at the right time. And these seemingly random people would come to help put what YCAB was doing into a nicer little package.

Many times I have felt like all the ingredients and spices were on the table, and that they were just waiting for a chef to come and cook a delicious dish. 'Chefs' have come from time to time in the span of YCAB's history, and it seems as though they come at just the right time, exactly when we need them.

※ ※ ※

I snapped my attention back to my slides and continued to describe each YCAB pillar in depth. I came to the education programme for school dropouts, which was born two or three years after the first pillar was launched. I said, 'I have to admit, though, that there was a lack of awareness at first on where to bring YCAB. When people look at YCAB today, they usually wonder how I came up with ideas and innovation for the programmes. To be fair, it wasn't like I had it all figured out since the very beginning. In fact, I didn't plan most of it. It came to me both organically and, in some cases, mysteriously.'

'Sometimes we make decisions in life and we don't understand why we make them; we don't have reasons, but then at some point they begin to make sense and bring certain goodness. There are things at play that lead us down a certain path. But to a casual observer, it seems like we have so brilliantly paved a certain path that now looks sparkling, great and predetermined,' I added.

'An example of this is the story of the birth of Rumah Belajar (learning centre), which began all the way back in early 2000. How it started was quite accidental in nature, but it unfolded nicely as though we had carefully planned it. It all started when one of my relatives, a second aunt and uncle from my mother's side of the family, approached us and asked us to buy their house in Duri Kepa, West Jakarta.

'"Vera, why don't you buy our house?" they asked. "It's getting too big for us now that the kids have gone out to work, and we want to live in a smaller house."

'We really didn't need a house at that time, but we went to look at the property anyway, out of respect for the senior members of the family.

'During that visit, we found out that the house had a unique shape to it. It was wider at the front than it was at the back. The best way to describe it would be trapezium-shaped, which was not auspicious, according to feng shui. *Ah, this must be the reason why this particular house hasn't sold even after being on the market for about two years,* I thought to myself.

'"Vera, you can just buy the house for however much you think it is worth. We just really want to move into a smaller house," my aunt said after we viewed the house and reviewed the paperwork. After giving it some thought, we ended up buying the property, even though at the time, we really had no use for it.

'Meanwhile, at that point in time, I started to learn more about the school-dropout rates in Indonesia. Dropping out of high school before graduating often leads teenagers to make uninformed lifestyle choices, such as engaging in unprotected sex, drug use, and so on. The same two results emerge: poverty, and lack of knowledge or skills. This seemed to be a pretty consistent reality. If children drop out of school, what are their chances of making the most of their lives? Of the 2 million Indonesian kids who did not finish high school, more than half of them dropped out due to financial problems. They reported public school was expensive: they needed to pay for tuition, books, and uniforms. At that point in time the free school programme did not yet exist; it was only established under our current president Joko Widodo.

'However, even now, when public schools are free, there are still associated costs with going to school; children still need transport money, for example. Therefore, affordability is the key to school attendance. All I could think of at that point was how important it was to give dropouts the opportunity to go back to school. At the same time, I also knew that these kids needed to have a set of skills to make them ready to compete in the job market. I thought that the best skills we could equip them with were basic computer skills and English literacy. Thinking about all of this led me to my "Eureka" moment: I would build a learning centre (Rumah Belajar). And, thanks to my aunt and uncle, I already had a property fit for the purpose!

'Sometimes, you don't really know what you're doing when you make certain decisions, but later on it almost feels like the decisions you made were predetermined. As result, something you never thought possible emerges; something like Rumah Belajar can be born out of it. A very good outcome indeed. When stars align, I believe that all things work together for good.

'I thought I was being charitable by helping a relative, but in fact they helped direct me onto a path that I was meant to follow. They helped me fulfil a need that I didn't realise even existed. Once I was made aware of the need for Rumah Belajar, the whole thing fell into place. I had the perfect property already. Though at first I felt slightly pressured into buying my aunt and uncle's house, somehow there were dots to be connected. Being pressured can sometimes inflict pain, too. It was amazing that this pain turned into joy, after finding the purpose of the inflicted pain in the first place.

'There was a need to help school dropouts and I had an empty *rumah* (house). We turned the bedrooms into classrooms and the other rooms into a library and common areas. We then thought of the name Rumah Belajar, which literally translates as "a house to study". It marked the birth of our second pillar, HoLD (House of Learning Development).'

I could sense the moderator's body language giving me the hint to move forward with my point about the sustainable innovation part of this education programme. Acknowledging this, I said, 'Let me finish my thought in thirty seconds and move on to the next phase of how we've managed to sustain this education programme. But first, here's what I realised,' I got excited with it and continued, 'If my aunt and uncle hadn't asked me to buy their house, would Rumah Belajar exist at all?'

'I knew that helping a relative should promote joy. But I still felt pressured into buying a property that we didn't need. One thing I learned from this particular experience is that being faithful to the calling to help others as much as we can really is its own reward. First, it gives us the opportunity to practise generosity. Second, we never know the good that can come out of it. For me, my aunt and uncle's request opened the door to YCAB's education pillar. As a result, more than 42,000 underprivileged youth were able to gain education and skills. Not only that, we also helped them secure employment upon the completion of their education course. That's how our education pillar was born.'

As if he couldn't help himself, the moderator interrupted me, 'Veronica, we have heard the story of how your education programmes came into being, now tell us more about how the economic empowerment arm came about. From what I have heard, therein lies YCAB's true innovation. Please tell us about this programme that is unique to YCAB.'

'Thank you for your great question. The third pillar is our economic empowerment pillar, which was born out of inspiration I got from my daughter, Adelle. Everything really does happen for a reason.' I started my next point while debating in my head whether to tell the short or long version. I decided it was important to tell the story just as I remembered it.

'I'd like to tell you about a day when quality time spent with my daughter Adelle turned out to be one of the most important days in determining the future of YCAB, and the future of so many people.

'"It's so good to have you back home, Mum. I've missed you so much," Adelle whispered in my ear while welcoming me back with a hug after a long-haul trip. As we separated I saw that she had a pretty serious look on her face as she said, "By the way, Mum, tomorrow it is your turn to chaperone us. All the other mums in my group have done it. You're the only one left. So can you? Please, please." How could I say no when she asked me so sweetly, fixing me with her brown puppy-dog eyes? No matter how tired I was, a "no" was not an option. I think all mothers have fallen under their little princess' spell before.

'Being an organised young lady, Adelle sat me down and began to explain everything. She told me that she was on a deadline to finish the data collection for her school project. It was part of her community service work in which she, as part of a group of four girls, had chosen to learn about microfinance. I was a little taken aback. I was quite surprised and obviously curious about how she and her group had picked microfinance as their main theme. I knew about Muhammad Yunus and his famous economic empowerment programme that won him a Nobel Prize but I thought to myself, *What made them choose this topic? What do they want to learn? What are they planning to do with the beneficiaries of microfinance?* Those were the questions bouncing around my mind as Adelle shared the plan for the next day. I nodded in agreement, although a bit dizzy from jet lag. I smiled, realising that I was looking at a miniature me – Adelle was so determined when she wanted something done.

'The next day, around eight in the morning, we were set to

go to Desa Leles – a village located about thirty minutes from Adelle's school in the Karawaci area, on the outskirts of Jakarta. Adelle was twelve then, but her ambition was way beyond her years.

'Marching through the village, Adelle and her group stopped at a simple house made from woven bamboo with an unfinished floor. In fact, there was no flooring. I found myself standing on the hardened red soil looking at very minimal furniture in a tiny room. The girls comfortably found their corner, and we all came together and sat on the floor that was covered with worn-out *tikar*, a hand-woven mat made of coconut leaves. The girls all had flip charts and pens, eager to take notes. They had prepared a list of questions and couldn't wait to interview the women, the beneficiaries of this particular microfinance programme.

'As I listened to the girls' line of questioning, I began to immerse myself in the daily lives of the people who lived in the village and the little money they earned every day. It felt like a cold slap to my face. I had read many articles about the widening gap between the rich and poor in Indonesia, but those are just words. When I read the population data and found the brutal truth that half of the Indonesian population still lived on under USD2 per day, that's knowledge. Then I did the maths and realised that half of the population meant more than 100 million people, that's statistics. But as I stood there face to face with villagers living in poverty, and heard their stories, the information came to life and the statistics became reality.

'I could hardly breathe trying to imagine how anyone could survive on so little. It wasn't just one person surviving on barely

IDR30,000 (approximately USD2.20) per day, it was the mother and two of her children: a whole family!

'I observed this lady as she was telling us how microfinance had helped her. She doesn't seem that old, I thought to myself, and with two young children around five and seven years old, she couldn't be older than forty. Her dark skin looked prematurely wrinkled, but there was something more in her face that I noticed. I saw a spark of simple hope. I also saw a sense of accomplishment and pride.

'That was dignity. And that dignity took her far beyond what she could imagine. With the small loan she had received, she was able to double her daily income. She continued her story, excitedly telling us that because of the loan, her children didn't have to walk an hour to school anymore. Her children could save forty minutes each way travelling to and from school, as she could now afford to give them money to take a *mikrolet* (small bus).

'My heart was squeezed and I felt a jolt in my stomach. Tears started to build up at the corners of my eyes. The reality of poverty was indeed brutal. I thought I knew about being poor. But this type of poverty really tore me apart. My heart was trembling because of more than what I had heard. I trembled because of the paradox I saw: I saw contentment in them, and gratefulness. They had almost nothing, yet they maintained their dignity.

'They continued to fight for their lives and they prevailed. It was the most powerful and beautiful thing to see that even with all their limitations, they were content. What G.K. Chesterton said came to my mind, "There are two ways to get enough. One is to accumulate more and more. The other is to desire less and less." I realised that poverty alone could not paralyse the human spirit; in many instances it actually empowered it. It was a very inspiring moment for me. It was a moment in my life that really humbled me.

'Adelle didn't know how my job as her chaperone that day had brought me to this new understanding. I didn't expect it, either. YCAB's microfinance programme later became its economic empowerment arm. It is our third programme pillar – HOpE – and it was born out of Adelle's school project.

'Neither of us knew that our morning in Desa Leles would change the lives of tens of thousands of low-income women who wouldn't have had the means to improve their daily income otherwise.'

I could sense that the energy of the room had changed by the time I finished my story. The female audience members were especially engaged with the story. I love how this story moves people, especially when I further explained how we later realised that giving access to small capital to the mothers of our students helped reduce the high attrition rate of students in Rumah Belajar.

For the longest time, Rumah Belajar had tried to help dropouts return to school, but we were still struggling with some students who needed to work and help make ends meet for their family's survival.

'Yes, we had many problems, but I felt like I was exposed to new opportunities, even a new possibility for YCAB's sustainability. I felt like the dots were finally aligned and ready to be connected.' I paused for a while, checking to see if the audience was still with me. Then I continued, 'After much deliberation, YCAB's microfinance programme was born six months after that 2009 trip to Desa Leles. The project was operating in full swing by 2010. Now, seven years down the road, we have reached out to almost 150,000 women. Our major goal is to extend capital to a quarter of a million women micro-entrepreneurs by 2020.

'Who would have thought that fulfilling one motherly duty could lead to this?' I said in closing. There was a second or two of pin-drop silence. I knew I had won the audience's hearts.

'Let me now show you this one last slide and then I'll give the floor back to you,' I said while signalling to the moderator that I was about to conclude. 'And perhaps I'll take a question or two after.'

I clicked onto my last slide. It was the one showing YCAB's model of change. This slide shows how through social investment programmes, YCAB provides micro capital for the mothers of students (and the other women micro-entrepreneurs in that community) with one important condition: they must keep their children in school as long as they are our clients. With the small capital we provide, we hope to stabilise their daily income and then improve it, so they can keep supporting their children's education. And once their education is sustained, we hope the children will graduate, find jobs and become self-reliant. We also hope that once they are established they will give back and invest through a mutual fund into our social investment bucket. With that, the whole cycle will be served and perpetuated.

PREMISE FOR CHANGE

Concluding the session, I thought it was important to sum things up and really drive home what makes YCAB stand out. 'The uniqueness of our programme is due to two factors. One, the access to capital is conditional. We make it this way because we believe that education is the one thing that can break the poverty cycle. Two, YCAB's microfinance is mission driven. We use microfinance as the means to an end, and the end we want to achieve is education for all.' Excited by my closing statement, I paused a little then concluded, 'The best part of all, is that it is sustainable. It's an innovative model that links financial inclusion and education to promote welfare.'

'Please give Veronica a round of applause. Thank you, Vera, that was really encouraging as well as inspiring,' said the moderator. I smiled and took a deep breath in relief, feeling grateful that the presentation had gone smoothly.

'Now let's move on to our Q&A session. I think we have time for a couple of questions?' the moderator asked. I answered with a nod.

As much as I love speaking about what I do, and sharing my vision, I think Q&A sessions make these presentations worthwhile. Worthwhile because when audience members ask questions or make comments, I know there is real interest and that they have connected with what I have said. And in many cases, I have seen meaningful support grow from the initial flush of interest.

Eager to answer my first question, I watched as a few hands were raised. The moderator pointed to one woman sitting in the middle row. After a short introduction, she asked, 'From your story, I feel like everything just fell into place nicely as you grew YCAB. I'm wondering if you've encountered challenges along the way? Perhaps you could share with us what the biggest challenge was in introducing and running the programme, as well as in running business units? And how does running a for-profit company differ from running a non-profit?'

As I tried to gather my thoughts together, the moderator nodded giving me the sign to start answering the question right away. Luckily, this was a frequently asked question and I had answered it many times before. It was an important question nonetheless, because a lot of people can learn a lot from it.

'Good question, thanks for that. Yes, I encountered many challenges during the development of YCAB Foundation, including the business units. Some of which were the best things that could have ever happened to me, because I would not have learnt if I didn't have to tackle those challenges. Let me give you a couple of examples of the challenges we faced at multiple levels to explain.

'At the programme level, during the first years of running the learning centre for the poor, we went through a steep learning curve. We had to tackle the four Ws and one H – the who, when, where, what and how.

'Remember at the beginning I briefly mentioned the high attrition rate? Well, there were many other problems we had to solve in order to operate effectively. Let me unpack each one.

'What we really wanted to do was to reach out to the kids who worked on the streets, and none of us had any experience running an education programme in the slum areas. The first thing we learned was to choose our ground carefully. We didn't know at that stage that there are many kinds of street kids: those who are "organised"; those who are just trying to make a living for their family; and then there are those who just hang out and sometimes make money in the streets, but earning money for their families is not their main goal.

'The first category is known as core street kids; they usually no longer have any attachment to their own family, but have a *mami* who organises their income and feeds them. The last two categories still maintain an attachment to their parents and family, and they will contribute any money they make to the family.

'The kids who still have some kind of attachment to their own families are the ones who are best suited to YCAB's programme. Although they bear some responsibility in earning for the family, they aren't the main breadwinners. The most difficult kids for us to work with are the core street kids. They just don't want to – or more accurately *won't* – go to school at the risk of being ridiculed and/or cast out by their *mami*. Once they leave their *mami*, they can't go back – they won't be welcome.

'I remember going under the Tomang Bridge in West Jakarta where there were a lot of the organised street kids. We held a few classes there, but it didn't work out well. There was so much fear in them. If they are not 100 per cent sure they will make it in class, they won't leave, preferring to stay at "home with *mami*".

'That's their biggest concern, while the problem on our end was that we didn't really have the capacity to "tame" them. Teaching them how to behave appropriately was much more difficult than teaching them their ABCs. The street kids who are still connected to their families are somewhat "tamer"; thus we work best with them.

'At that point in time, we still lacked the tools to determine which kids would benefit from our programme. We indeed needed more resources for recruitment. So we came up with a better screening process and, with that in place, we began to admit those who are eager to learn. By doing this we managed to bring down the turnover rate from fifty to sixty per cent to ten to fifteen per cent. It's not perfect, but it means we still have room for improvement. What makes us really happy is of those who complete the programme, 100 per cent pass the national exam at the end.

'Once we had resolved the screening process, we faced another challenge: location. Like any other venture, finding the right location is crucial. We needed density. We needed enough school-age kids within a five-kilometre radius to attend Rumah Belajar to avoid too much expense in running the programme.

'We felt that we were ineffective at the beginning and that was the price we had to pay while we learnt. When the cost per student was brought down to half, the pain turned into pleasure. It is truly my deep pleasure to see how many Rumah Belajar centres we have established over the course of time. It took us six years to set up three centres, but since then, seventy-seven Rumah Belajar have been established across the archipelago, including five outside of Indonesia. To date more than 40,000 youth have gone through one or more programmes at Rumah Belajar.

'So we overcame three challenges: one, we learned that we needed to have clear targets and to realise that we cannot help everyone, we can only can help those who want to help themselves; two, screening is important to ensure students' academic success; and three, the importance of being in the right location to help lower the cost per student.

'But that's not all. Picking the right children and having the right screening tools do not solve the economic problem. We needed to figure out how the children could afford the associated costs of attending Rumah Belajar. Transport, for example.

'Until Adelle took me to Desa Leles, we didn't know what the solution was. By offering the students' mothers a small amount of capital in support of their micro businesses, their daily income increased – doubled or tripled in some cases after twelve or fifteen months of intervention. Only once we are sure that the family income is stabilised can we be certain that they have the means to send their kids to school.

'However, no matter how good the education programme is, enabling students to be independent after they finish school is the one thing that makes our investment worthwhile. Watching the graduates become *mandiri* (independent) is a great feeling. But knowing our investment in their education makes them self-reliant, that is what gives us the greatest joy. That's our job done.

'So, the lesson we learned from running education programmes for the poor is this: there's a very close link between education and economic empowerment. This deepened our understanding about how to best serve the people at the bottom of the pyramid.'

I glanced at the moderator; judging from his body language he had something to say, 'It's great that you have shared in depth the challenges at the programme implementation level, but what about other challenges at the enterprise level?'

'Most of YCAB's business units are quite sustainable. Each has a business model that generates enough income to profit. Some took eight years to turn a profit, some as little as a year. I am very grateful for that.

'The biggest challenge is always the people. How do we raise up an army of dedicated people who want to work towards YCAB's mission? Getting YCAB's core values and mission into hearts and minds is the most difficult challenge. It takes us years; in fact we are still working things out, layer by layer to embed the mission and values into their souls. As an enterprise, working capital is a challenge we face from time to time, but it's relatively easy to deal with once we can work with commercial rate financing.

'Above all else though, what I'd like to share with you here is how we dealt with failure. C.S. Lewis once said that failures – repeated failures – are signposts on the road to achievement. One fails forward toward success. YCAB's evolution is a perfect example of that quote's meaning.

'Much like the cycle of development of a child from birth to maturity, YCAB had to be born, then learn to crawl and pick itself up after falling down, before learning to walk and eventually run.

'Everything was surely not all perky and peachy. We failed, too, from time to time. One of our business units, Pelangi, which was established in 2004, didn't quite make it. There are some situations in life that you cannot fix, and it's better to start over, start fresh. When a company is no longer making money and fails to be commercially viable, then one must have the courage to admit defeat and pull the plug and begin again.

'Pelangi was the second company we established to help support YCAB's programmes. Pelangi was an abbreviation of Pelatihan Anak dan Guru Indonesia, which loosely translates as the Centre for Youth and Teacher Training. The idea was to provide training programmes for teachers. It seemed like a great idea, but the sad reality was that of the many schools we approached, none were willing to send their teachers for training, let alone sign a contract with us so that we could provide teacher training. All of them thought IDR250,000 per training programme per teacher was too expensive. That was only around USD20! The schools preferred to do the training in-house, even though they knew it was usually done in an unstructured fashion. Since we were unsuccessful in convincing the schools to send their teachers for training, we decided to offer training packages for corporations. Here we found a better connection. The businesses understood the benefit of employee training and they were willing to pay. So corporate training was our cash cow for the first few years, and helped to subsidise the teacher training so we could offer it at a much lower cost.

'The other business stream we had was SuperCamp, a leadership and academic excellence camp for teenagers, offered at premium prices. I really liked running camps like these and the participants learned so many skills that helped them to do much better academically. We offered speed-reading classes and memorisation classes among others. However, after several camps, we felt that this business wasn't sustainable. It was actually a franchise model, so we ended up making almost nothing while the franchisor enjoyed a much better margin.

'Basically, both Pelangi and SuperCamp were charitable works for us; YCAB wasn't earning anything from them. Something was seriously wrong with those business models! It took courage to admit that we had failed, that things hadn't happened the way we wanted, the way we planned. We thought we needed to give the company a break while working things out and finding the right fit and the right business model. Years later, the relaunch of Pelangi was a success and it made a profit in its first year. Pelangi has been rebranded as Flip. The new name was inspired by our experience: things can 'flip' drastically when the business model is clear and the right business leader is in place. Now Bobby Hartanto and Shasha Disyacitta are running the company and their passion and deep understanding of the sector has really helped the business to flourish.

'As I look back, one of the key things we learnt was that we needed to be clear about who was running the show. This is the answer to the last part of your question,' I said while glancing at the first questioner. 'You asked me the difference between running non-profit and for-profit entities. It's not really different at all; both require professionalism and passion. But for me personally, it is clear now that I must stick with YCAB, and the appointment of someone to be the head of the company is crucial. I shouldn't even play a part in selecting the management team, as they need to have good chemistry between them and should be selected by the head of the company, not me.

'Also, I learned that very talented people can be prevented from delivering their best if they work under unfit leadership. Not because they cannot do the job well, but simply because they are not in a conducive environment.

'Potential can remain just that: potential. If potential is not nurtured it won't result in actual success. It would be quite sad if we missed out on successful results and our workers missed out on their chance to shine. This can happen when people are not placed in positions based on their competency and skill level; they can end up in the wrong place and be given tasks they are not passionate about. For instance, people who were good at delivering materials ended up doing managerial tasks.

'Reflecting on all this, I am convinced that failure itself is not the worst thing. The worst thing is when one fails without knowing why. One needs to understand the value in failing, and rising from the ashes. Having the courage to start over is a virtue. But the biggest lesson of all is that failure needs to be celebrated as much as success does. The pain failure brings is only temporary, but the pleasure it brings when we rise up again is very long lasting.

'Sometimes I compare my journey growing YCAB to walking in a dark alley with a lantern in my hand. As I take one step, the lantern will brighten the area around me and light up my immediate path. But I cannot see the end of the alley, the light from my lantern does not shine that far. But I think the willingness to take each step is important, especially when we do it without knowing what's going to happen. Each step is a step of faith; as I go further I believe that people or "chefs" are sent to help light up a particular spot, to help light up the alley one step at a time. And as wonderful and easy as everything may seem from the outside, it takes faith and courage to pave a new way.'

'This is all very fascinating, to learn raw facts from a practitioner like you, Veronica. But I'm afraid our time is running out, but we have just under five minutes for one last question,' the moderator said. 'Please be brief in your question and the response,' he continued while picking a young woman from the audience.

'Hi Veronica, my name is Stephanie. I have heard your in-depth work on YCAB Foundation, I must commend you on this amazing work you do. But I am curious to know more about how you define "impact". I've seen the remarkable number of people you have reached through YCAB's programmes over the last eighteen years. Three million is a huge number to achieve. But what really keeps you going? I'm sure at the end of the day we all want to see a transformation, a change that we can bring to the world. Can you tell us more about your impact and how you define it?'

I quickly got excited with the question and responded, 'Yes, impact is the ultimate question one should ask about,' I paused, debating which angle I should take to keep my response brief. Then I said, 'It is not easy to define it. One school of thought is more into quantifying impact through something that they call SROI – social return on investment – while the more humanistic school of thought prefers to use the qualitative approach. Qualitative data is usually collected through stories, capturing the human side of it.

'The 3 million people we reached is surely a big number, that's quantitative data. It gives you the breadth of programmes, how many are exposed to it. Some experts debate that quantitative data is just output. It's not exactly the outcome, it doesn't detail the actual impact of a programme. To some, the number of people affected is equal to output. For example, 100 students come to study at Rumah Belajar, that's the output. Of those 100, if ninety people graduate and pass national exams – that's outcome. Subsequently, the impact is assessed from the number of graduated students who get jobs and become financially independent in the one or two years following their graduation, depending on when we cut off the time for impact. Impact such as this is known as depth.

'On the other hand, there are others who do not mind qualifying the number of people reached by the programme as impact. Simple. So you can see that the word impact is used so extensively to the point it's confusing. But YCAB wants both. We want both breadth and depth in order to show impact. Let me tell you a couple of stories that always move me. I think they demonstrate real impact at its best.

'One of our students had dropped out of school when she was fifteen. She later enrolled in and graduated from Rumah Belajar. Her name is Roro Risnawati, and she's now twenty-four years old. After graduation, Roro managed to secure employment with one of YCAB's business units called Beauty Inc.

'Founded in 2007, Beauty Inc. is a beauty clinic specialising in non-invasive treatments using FDA-approved technology in radio frequency, laser, and mesotherapy. It employs YCAB's graduates who have learned the skills needed to be a beautician or spa therapist.

'Roro initially studied at a public SMK (vocational school), which is equivalent to a high school level. One year into the programme, a tragedy hit her family: her father lost his job and abandoned them. Her family's financial condition has worsened ever since. Even though Roro was offered a scholarship by her previous school, the transportation costs were still a huge obstacle. Moreover, her mother who had been working as a laundress was the family's only breadwinner. Her family was buried deep in debt.

'There were times when Roro had to walk for an hour to get home from school because she didn't have enough money to take public transport. Roro had to give up SMK, but was determined to find alternative education. Then she found Rumah Belajar, which was close to her house.

'With a strong desire to learn, Roro quickly acquired the knowledge and skills needed for her current job. With her income from Beauty Inc, she started to save and when she had enough money, she pulled together all her resources to pay for her university tuition. She is now studying at STMIK Indonesia, a pretty good IT college. She is taking an information systems course, majoring in programming. She achieved a very good GPA, and I encouraged her to apply for a YCAB scholarship. She did, and she's now one of the brightest stars, both at the university and at work.

'Today, Roro's life has totally changed. Her family is debt-free. She no longer has to choose between paying transportation or buying a meal. She no longer dreams of being successful, she *is* successful. She doesn't wait for opportunities to come to her, she's creating opportunities through her perseverance and hard work. She is now the main breadwinner in her family, and her mother is extremely proud of her.'

I could see some of the audience members had actually leaned forwards in their seats as I was telling the story. That usually happens when people get more interested; a human story always results in deeper attention. While I had everyone engrossed, I continued and said, 'Let me close with another story that just came to my attention and I personally think is more dramatic than Roro's.

'There's a girl called Kristanti. She was a domestic helper or maid who was responsible for all the housekeeping and childcare at a home that was located near one of YCAB's Rumah Belajar. She asked permission from her boss to attend Rumah Belajar and get her high school diploma. When she graduated, YCAB had just started a new programme in partnership with Samsung that taught young people skills in electronics repair. Kristanti could see that the programme offered the opportunity to learn a valuable vocational skill and joined the first batch of students. She was the only female in the class and she achieved the best marks and graduated at the top of the class. She was subsequently offered a job with Samsung as a result of her excellent performance, and here comes the big bang: in 2014 she was named Samsung's best employee in Indonesia and in 2016 she was the best Samsung customer service agent in Southeast Asia!'

I could hear immediate applause, as if the whole room was joining me in my sense of pride. Every time it happens, I know I'm doing something right. This is it, a fulfilment of my calling.

'Our holistic youth-development programme, through our three pillars, HeLP, HoLD, and HOpE, has made this possible. Everything makes sense. We HeLP youth; HoLD them for some time while educating them; and we give them real HOpE in their lives. It all makes perfect sense now, that youth development is the answer.

'It is truly a wonderful and fulfilling moment when we see

someone like Roro or Kristanti become who they really are, achieving their full potential. I believe it is not those who are poor who do not have a future; it is those who have no dreams who do not have a future. Roro is no longer poor because she continued to dream; she now has the means to make her dreams a reality, and we are all very proud of Kristanti and her career achievements.' I paused a little before making my closing statement. 'And, that, ladies and gentlemen, is the real impact. Impact that brings change and transformation to someone's life.'

I could hear the voice of the moderator closing the session, and with it, the talk, followed by the audience applauding and then some classical music started to play softly in the background. I could see some of the audience members coming towards the panellists, lining up to speak with us. I could see the lady who asked the first question approaching, as I began a conversation with a man who had happened to reach me first.

'No school and no education means no future. Vulnerability is what we fight against. The answer to vulnerability is empowerment.'

5
chapter

GIVE UNTIL IT HURTS

Glancing at my watch, I saw that it was almost four in the afternoon. I had just endured a four-hour car ride on a non-existent road from Gunungsitoli, the capital of Nias island, following a four-hour flight from Jakarta to Sitoli with a short transit in Medan. Finally, we arrived at Sirombu on the west coast of the island, off northern Sumatra. It had been pouring hard with rain that morning, and the sky was still grey with a touch of light blue, reminding me that the island had been badly hit by the massive Boxing Day tsunami that killed thousands and destroyed hundreds of houses. I could still feel the chill inside my bones when I landed there just a month or two after the gigantic tsunami ransacked this part of Sumatra. I could still smell the death and see the gloomy faces of survivors. Their sense of trauma was so real, it was infectious and it scarred my soul. Those eyes seemed helpless, yet resilient enough for me to have a strong desire to rebuild their lives. But I didn't even know where to begin to help.

Through a consortium of the Monaco Asia Society, United in Diversity (UID), the Zero to One Foundation and YCAB, it was decided to do something tangible. We decided to work hand in hand to carry out a reconstruction project, united to help the people of Sirombu by rebuilding their community. YCAB facilitated the process of rebuilding by purchasing the land for the new buildings in an area further back from the coast. The land was still close to the beach but on higher ground.

The new land was given to the victims of the tsunami and their families, and around 250 new houses were built, along with a K–12 school facility and a community centre. The once destitute district of Sirombu had finally begun to breathe new life again. *This is how it's supposed to be*, I thought to myself, looking around and observing my surroundings. I was pleased with what I saw. Houses were nicely laid out, uniformly painted and furnished, and powered by solar panels. Now all the families here were sheltered safely, children were playing and laughing, and mothers were nursing babies and providing meals for their families. It was certainly a heartwarming sight. For a minute there, at best, it made me forget about how horrible the weather had been all day, and how tiring the journey to get there had been, and how the project was almost stopped due to nine-point earthquakes that struck the island again and again in the midst of construction. I remember this made all our workers from Java whom we sent there to reinforce the local men scatter to the

This photo was taken a few days before my mum passed away. We turned her hospital room into a temporary photo studio to fulfil her wish for a final family photo. I am grateful that Mum was given the opportunity to see and make her selection from the photo proofs, thanks to our dear friend Marsio, the photographer, who rushed the process for her. To add extra poignancy to this photo, I actually turned thirty that day. I had such mixed feelings of about embracing a new decade of my life while losing my mum at the same time.

Mum and Dad in front of the church on the day of Dad's baptism on 2 June 1985. Dad became a Christian a few weeks after his supernatural experience. This is probably the last photo they had together before his demise in 1991. This is my favourite photo of them together, looking so radiant and peaceful.

Prague, June 1985. My first and last Europe trip with Mum and Dad. It was such a treat for us, and we made wonderful memories to cherish for life. It was a very impressive holiday by our standards then; I still have no clue how Dad had pulled together his limited resources for the trip. We travelled from Brussels down to Monte Carlo, visiting other countries in between, including the UK, France and the Netherlands.

ABOVE LEFT: This photo was taken in 1977 on the front porch of my childhood house located in the west of Jakarta. I was five years old.

ABOVE RIGHT: This photo was taken in 1992, one year after Dad passed away, in our house in Green Ville.

BELOW: A complete family photo taken in 1975.

TOP: The winners of the United Nations Civil Society Awards in 2001 along with the Minister of Foreign Affairs (centre); to her left is the Mayor of the city of Austria and to her right is the Under-Secretary-General of the United Nations.

BOTTOM: A photo from the early years of YCAB during which Mum was still active in supporting the foundation. From left to right: Aunt Greta (the wife of the Indonesian ambassador to Czechoslovakia during our visit in 1988), me, Chris Lasut, Sesanty Matulessy, Dr Andy Hukom (YCAB's Secretary-General from 2003–2015) and Mum.

TOP: YCAB used to hold the annual Lights On campaign, involving thousands of people including celebrities and volunteers. The photo was taken in 2005. Shown here are YCABers alongside volunteers in the city centre, known as HI Circle.

BOTTOM: A typical Rumah Belajar classroom. These young students dropped out of primary school but here they have the opportunity to continue their education through the 'Paket A' programme, which is equivalent to primary school.

TOP: Prince Albert of Monaco officiating the opening of new housing and a community centre in Sirombu, Nias – a tsunami-devastated area just off the tip of North Sumatra. More than 250 houses were built on higher ground, only a few hundred metres from where the previous coastal homes had stood. This housing rebuilding project was the first to be inaugurated for the victims of the 2004 Boxing Day tsunami.

BOTTOM: The United in Diversity (UID) team led by Cath Widjaja (centre, in white top) with Frans and Gina Sugiarta and Boyke Aveanto squatting in front of her.

I am very proud of Agung (left), a graduate of the first batch of Rumah Belajar Batik, which teaches traditional Indonesian cloth painting. His trainer and motivator, Purwanto (centre) shows off Agung's work. Agung has become a very successful batik artist and entrepreneur, earning a good income of at least triple the local minimum wage of USD100 per month.

A typical *blusukan* day, where I come and spend time talking to the beneficiaries of YCAB's mission-driven microfinance programme. *Blusukan* is when we talk to the people we serve in order to better understand their needs. On this special day, I took a group of Leica photographers who were on a journey to create a photo narrative book for YCAB, titled *Angel of Change*. I was also accompanied by Indonesia's most famous TV host, Andy Noya (seated on my right, wearing a baseball cap).

World Economic Forum on East Asia
Jakarta, 19-21 April 2015

TOP RIGHT: Me taking a role in speaking and moderating a session at the World Economic Forum on East Asia in Jakarta, Indonesia in 2015.

TOP LEFT: My two mentors, Khun Chai (right) and Sandro Calvani (left) at the Bangkok Global Dialogue on Sustainable Development in October 2013. Their spirit and wisdom will always inspire me. I love the energy whenever they are around. They are true examples of humanitarian warriors.

BOTTOM: Receiving the Schwab Foundation's Social Entrepreneur award from Mrs Hilde Schwab in Tianjin, China, on 11 September 2012. I became a 'Schwabbie' right after my graduation from the World Economic Forum's Young Global Leader class of 2006.

This photo was taken in the early days of YCAB. Megawati Soekarnoputri, who was then the Vice President of the Republic of Indonesia, at the inauguration of the National Narcotics Board of Indonesia, which YCAB helped organise on 11 September 2000.

I was part of the *Jokowi Relawan* team – a group of volunteers led by Abdee Negara, a very well known musician who became Jokowi's closest ally. Our group held the game-changing stadium rally that helped win Jokowi the presidency. This photo was taken during the breaking of fast event in the month of Ramadan at the Presidential Palace in Bogor, 2015.

ABOVE: The future of YCAB is in the hands of these young people, who are the members of YCAB Young Advisory Board. From left to right: Aditya Percaya (legal and international relations), Shasha Disyacitta (human capital development), Clairine Runtung (fundraising), Veronica Colondam, Iman Usman (content development) and Fransnico Susanto (web design developer).

BELOW: Board members at YCAB's Global Annual Meeting held in Jakarta, 2016.

point of no return.

Looking at the sunset sky, the natives of the land who read the signs of the clouds were telling me to prepare for another downpour at night. *Brace yourself, Vera. You can do this ... you can sleep on that floor and pray the night will be short.* I chanted those words to myself until I fell asleep. I could still hear a couple of men – the leaders of the village and some of our team including Pieter – talking outside planning a minute-by-minute rundown to welcome Prince Albert of Monaco. My strength was leaving me, the long journey and the brutal weather had taken its toll. My fatigue prevented me from participating in the last preparation meeting. I chose to visit the slumber land early instead.

※ ※ ※

'Let's do a little round to check on the houses nearby, just in case Prince Albert wants to come and visit. He should be arriving in a couple of hours, we still have time to do this,' I said to the United in Diversity team led by my good friend, Cath Widjaja, the next morning. We were all tired and cold. None of us had any appetite to eat anything that morning, especially after waking up surrounded by puddles of water from the rain; all of us were worried. *What if the entire complex is now muddy and messy? How can we clean the entire complex up to make it worthy of the Prince's inspection?* I could smell trouble.

'Can you help gather up some of these boys to dry up this area here, please?' I said to the superintendent while pointing to a part of the community centre that was a bit flooded due to the uneven floor. Not only did I want to make sure that the area was neat and dry, we also needed to show respect and appreciation to Prince Albert by keeping the area clear of water for safety reasons.

To my surprise, this middle-aged man snapped back at me in an overtly hostile tone, 'Why do we have to clean it? Let the Prince see the puddle so he knows that the building needs some more fixing. Aren't you happy to receive more money from the Prince? Besides, you might have built us the entire complex, but you didn't give us brooms and cleaning cloths. How can we clean this place up now?'

Those words were piercing to our ears and one of our teammates began to cry out of frustration and despair. The man's statement rendered me speechless for a moment, and anyone who knows me knows that I am never lost for words! But the man kept staring at us with a blank and hollow look on his face while a small crowd started to gather behind him. It was disturbing. I looked at him in disbelief. I looked at all the faces behind him, and thought to myself, *I can't believe these people, how ungrateful.* I experienced a slight pain in my chest; I didn't know if I was angry, disappointed, or sad in the face of this brutal reality. I actually didn't know how to react, so I chose to walk away. I needed reinforcements. Then Pieter came to the rescue.

He gathered up all the teenagers and showed them a stack of IDR 10,000 notes (each note worth approximately USD0.80). He waved the money at them. I saw the teens begin to line up for the cash, and once the money was in their pockets they began to clean. They dried the floor with whatever cloth they could get their hands on. Some actually used the shirts they were wearing. I had to walk away from this awful scene. *It's just ridiculous. We built all this for them, all brand new. This is the best deal ever. They can keep their old land and this new land is given free with a house on it – all furnished and powered by solar energy – what else could they want from us?*

I withdrew from the community centre so I could take a breather. The facade of the centre seemed so brand new, even the smell of new paint still lingered. Yet the energy of the community it sheltered was not right. There was something else missing aside from gratitude. It was a sense of ownership. *How can they not appreciate the fact that this is their property now?* I pondered. *They're the ones who will live here, not us. They've got to take care of it.* But I guess just because I think a certain way about something doesn't mean others will think the same way. I knew right there and then that God was trying to teach me something by giving me this experience.

It was a lesson I wouldn't have understood except that I had previously made a journey to the Indian city of Kolkata on one of my mission trips to the Missionaries of Charity – a congregation established by Mother Teresa. There was a room where nuns and volunteers as well as visitors could pay respect to the late Mother Teresa and in that solemn yet simple room there was a humble sign on the wall. There it was written 'Give Until It Hurts'. That phrase threw me into years of personal spiritual contemplation about what it means to truly give.

❋ ❋ ❋

I do not believe one can settle how much we ought to give. I am afraid the only safe rule is to give more than we can spare. In other words, if our expenditure on comforts, luxuries, amusements, etc., is up to the standard common among those with the same income as our own, we are probably giving away too little. If our charities do not at all pinch or hamper us, I should say they are too small. There ought to be things we should like to do and cannot do because our charitable expenditures exclude them.

C.S. Lewis

I didn't know what really caused the uncomfortable feeling in me that crowded afternoon in Kolkata. So many people were buzzing around on the street; everyone was busy with their own thing, minding their own business. That's a sight I had never encountered in my life. *This is how it looks*, I thought to myself, *if one third of a city's population lives on the streets. Does this city not have a government? How can they let their people live this way? Can anyone do something about this?* Negating my own thoughts, I continued to ponder, *To be honest though, how can anybody do anything when faced with 5 million homeless? Every contribution or idea would seem so small, so ineffectual in the face of such overwhelming poverty. Why haven't I read about this before?*

While I was trying to digest this new reality, I saw a couple of Bentleys and Benzes cruising down the very same street, elegantly oblivious to the poverty outside their windows. In one car I saw well-dressed men and women inside, busy with their cell phones; and in the other was seated a couple of youngsters, each with headphones in their ears, comfortably listening to their music. I wondered what was going on in their minds. How did their hearts become so hardened that they didn't acknowledge what was happening just outside their car window? Couldn't they see it? Didn't they care?

My eyes swept along the street one more time. Disturbingly I saw many half-naked people bathing under butterfly hydrants on both sides of the road. Some were still covered with shampoo bubbles, some were brushing their teeth and some women wrapped in their rather shabby looking saris sat comfortably on the street's side in the midst of dust. They were cooking food for their children, some of whom were impatiently waiting in front of their mother's pot, while others chased one another happily. In the midst of all that, I saw people selling dust-covered fruit and vegetables, some ready food and such. I don't remember the name of that long street, but if I had to name it I would call it Public Service Street. That street provided all kinds of facilities for the poor: water, shelter, even a livelihood. For as far as my eyes could see through the smudged windows of the bus, the scene remained pretty much the same. The window glass separated me from the visceral reality of the streets as I made my way to Mother Teresa's centre of ministry.

In the midst of the hot and humid weather of Kolkata, sweat started to roll down my neck into the collar of my loose white linen shirt. I tried rolling up my sleeves but the heat of the sun stung so aggressively that I changed my mind and decided to endure the heat for the sake of an even skin tone. Luckily, I didn't eat much during my seven-hour flight from Jakarta to Kolkata; if I had my discomfort would have been worse. The smell of burnt skin from the heat of the sun and sweat mixed with dirt, laundry detergent and the pollution smell of the city certainly didn't help. I took some deep breaths and gulped some water that I had in my bag to stay hydrated. Soon enough, I was feeling a lot better.

I had to feel better because this trip was very important. My aim was to visit the Mother House, a facility run by Mother Teresa's Missionaries of Charity to take care of the poorest of the poor. I had come not just for a visit but to be in the very place where her unending love for the dying made her worthy of the Nobel Peace Prize. I wanted to be there, to feel and to capture the devoted energy of love that the nuns have faithfully maintained since Mother Teresa's demise.

My decision to come to Mother House was long overdue, and once I arrived I felt slightly overwhelmed. I have had a huge respect for Mother Teresa all my life, but to be present in this particular spot in Kolkata where she served made me feel very emotional. When I got there, my admiration elevated. I didn't have enough time to explore the city of Kolkata before I visited the Mother House. I wish I did though, because I wanted to see and experience the many artistic rituals of India, especially because of the contrast between the rich and poor who co-exist in the city of Kolkata. After all, Kolkata is ranked the 12th richest city in the Asia-Pacific region, having recorded a 171 per cent increase in the number of super rich, according to *The Times of India* in 2015. It is comparable to Indonesia, as noted by *The Guardian* in 2017, where the total wealth of the top four richest people is equal to the worth of the 100 million poorest. What a huge and horrifying gap.

Driving through the city looking at my surroundings, there was a rustic, quiet charm, a sweet nostalgic empathy that I felt observing the neighbourhood. Each building contained some sort of an interior narrative that I'd find echoing in other parts of the world. I just couldn't really tell exactly where. The British East India Company arrived in 1690 and with that began the recorded history of Kolkata along with the coalescence of British and Indian cultures. Though the British moved the capital to New Delhi in 1911, Kolkata continued to be the centre for revolutionary organisations associated with the Indian Independence Movement.

I wondered what that independence had meant to India's Dalits, the lower than the lowest caste. The Dalits or 'untouchables' live below the four Hindu castes of Brahmin priests and teachers, Kshatriya warriors and rulers, Vaishya traders and Shudra servants, and they have suffered routine violence and discrimination for centuries. The word 'untouchables' literally means they cannot be touched; those who touch them will be 'unclean' for one or more days. To make matters worse, the Dalits are banned from drinking water from wells used by higher castes. They are also excluded from Hindu temples, and their children are forced to eat separately at school. Fighting for or demanding equal rights would mean eviction from their homes or being made outcasts. Hardly any of them have a government job, while their literacy rates are among the very lowest in the whole country. Nevertheless, two of India's presidents have been Dalits. That made me wonder, *I am sure those presidents shook hands with many people and why didn't they mind?*

What Mother Teresa did was to care for all needy people, including the Dalits. Oftentimes they are found dead in the streets of Kolkata and nobody would do anything to remove the bodies, let alone give them a proper burial. But the Mother House retrieves the bodies for burial and cares for those who are still alive. Missionaries of Charity's mission is also there to care for the hungry, the naked, the homeless, the crippled, the blind, the lepers, and all those people who feel unwanted, unloved and uncared for by the rest of society.

I wiped my sweaty forehead and drank some more water, trying to immerse myself in the tale and the history of this somehow dark yet magical city. Rajiv Gandhi, the Prime Minister of India from 1984 to 1989, referred to Kolkata as the 'dying city' because of the social and political traumas it had endured. I was finally able to figure out that it was the contrast between the rich cultural narration and the poverty I saw on the streets on Kolkata that made the city so memorable even now. Kolkata was captivating in her own ways.

From a distance, I spotted a grey four-storey building with brown shuttered windows marked with a small wooden sign, and I knew I had reached my destination. It was not a long walk from where the bus had dropped us, but that path felt so much longer when walking in the heat while navigating the muddy terrain under my feet. *I regret my choice of footwear*, I thought to myself, *I should've worn my sneakers. What was I thinking putting on a pair of flip flops?*

As I walked along the narrow lane running along the left side of the Mother House, I could picture the late Mother Teresa in a white sari with blue trim as she ventured into the streets with a noble mission: to serve Christ by tending to the poorest of the poor. Mother Teresa was determined that no one should die unwanted on the streets. What a beautiful Godly vision.

Entering the initial doorway, the corridor opened up with a few potted plants, a statue of Mary, and also a statue of Mother Teresa. It was still early, around ten in the morning, when I arrived at the Mother House, but already I saw some volunteers soaked in sweat, hand-washing and disinfecting dirty laundry, while others were bathing patients and helping them take pills and food, while yet another group of volunteers distributed morning snacks. There were volunteers from all over the world, including Japan, Spain, America, Canada, Italy, France, Germany, and Ireland. Not all of them were young, some of them were actually in their prime, and some older, well beyond retirement age. Later, I learned that many patients had tuberculosis and, according to one of the doctors I talked to there, it was something of which the volunteers had to be cautious. It was recommended that they limit their contact with these patients and allow the permanent medical team to handle them.

The faint smell of chai, perhaps from the breakfast earlier that morning, and disinfectant filled the room full of patients, volunteers, doctors, and nuns. A small courtyard gave an escape from the mixed smell and gave a sense of openness and fresh air to the entire place.

'Good morning. I hope I am not interrupting. I am visiting from Jakarta, Indonesia. Do you mind if I ask you a few questions?' I asked a volunteer who didn't seem too busy with his chore. He nodded with his eyes, ready to make conversation, so I continued, 'How did you end up here and how long have you been volunteering?'

'I came from France and I have been here for three days and I'll be here for two weeks. It took me years to get here, to become a volunteer. Apparently, they have a really long waiting list.' From our short conversation I also learned that he was a senior surgeon, and while he was attending to patients at the house, rarely a day passed without a resident passing away. Most of the time it was the duty of the volunteers to drag sick, dying and dead people inside the home. Rather upset and troubled by what he had told me, I thanked him for his time before he left to attend a patient, carefully examining her stomach. Apparently, they had found a tumour in her stomach and it was already as big as a tennis ball. I saw him scribble some notes and then move on to a very weak-looking old lady.

From where I stood observing him, I could smell the unpleasant odour emanating from this corner. The volunteer doctor wore a dark blue full-body plastic apron that looked sturdy and it came in handy when he had another patient in his arms as he tried to feed her with some liquid food. *What an amazing sight. This is real compassion. He doesn't need to do that, but he's here for that.* I felt the corner of my eyes fill with tears while my heart experienced a strange sensation of ecstasy, witnessing such compassion. It was refreshingly inspiring. Then I looked around and I saw everyone was busy, almost each patient had one caretaker. Such was the usual morning at the Nirmal Hriday, Home for the Destitute and the Dying, also known as Kalighat, one of the nine homes within the organisation that I visited. Such a blessed house. God bless Mother Teresa.

One of the senior nuns approached me as I was making my way across the courtyard. As she was guiding me upstairs, the nun took me to visit the little museum where they had laid Mother Teresa's body to rest before her burial. I could see the entire wall was filled with a photo narrative showing a young Mother Teresa before she came to India, all the way up to her Nobel acceptance speech. I began to better understand how her ministry really mattered to the world, and even more now. The nun explained to me the hierarchy of the nunnery and how they dealt with the succession issue following Mother Teresa's demise. While listening to her, I couldn't help but scan the entire complex below me. I saw a group of young people gathered around listening to a briefing from another nun. When the nun explaining the succession issues to me paused, I took the opportunity to ask what the group of people was doing and who they were. She told me that they were a new batch of volunteers who would stay for the following week or month. They came from many countries and usually there was a waiting period of a year or two before they could come and volunteer. I thought it was very impressive that the volunteers were committed enough to wait that long. I was even more impressed that they stayed after I saw the sleeping quarters for the volunteers. To my mind they were so modest that they were almost unliveable.

Absorbing all the information and keeping it tight in my heart, I left Kalighat. Almost an hour later, I arrived at the Home for Children – Nirmala Shishu Bhavan – another one of the homes at Mother House that was established in 1955 for abandoned street babies and children. It was rather appalling to see such a big room filled with rows and rows of cots and little babies. I looked downstairs and saw some toddlers, between the ages of two and five years old, most of whom had physical or mental disabilities. 'Many of these children are street children whose parents can't afford to raise them. Most are abandoned because of mental health issues and/or physical disabilities. This seems to be a huge problem in India: parents not wanting special needs children, especially children with double disabilities,' explained the main sister in charge. I felt really sorry for the children, but at the same time I understood the limitations of their impoverished parents. I just wished things were different.

It was heart-wrenching to witness two families, each with a baby who was to be handed into the sisters' care. They couldn't afford the children and they didn't know how to care for special needs babies. I was grief-stricken at the loss and parting. And just as there were goodbyes, there were also very rare introductions. Adoptive parents would come into the playground and cuddle and bond with their future children. But then to see the faces and the reactions of other children who had nobody visiting them was even more heartbreaking. I couldn't imagine how hard it was for the sisters and the volunteers who had to constantly cope with these sad scenes.

I thought about my children who live with a lot of privileges and built-in love, and how fortunate it is that they can grow up and have more options and opportunities in life than any of these poor children will ever have. Yet, on the flip side, there are kids who are born with a lot of privileges yet decide to throw them all away. The latter is sadder, I think. This forlorn thought took me back to a few years ago when I visited an institution in Jakarta; it was the experience that acted as a catalyst in the creation of YCAB.

※ ※ ※

I remember experiencing a rather eerie moment followed by a painful feeling as I walked along the hallway of a big ward of the psychiatric hospital where patients mingled. I saw mixed feelings of desperation, frustration and a tint of entrapment in the eyes of these young patients. Some of them looked okay, some tired and many were just hopeless, staring into oblivion while puffing away on their cigarettes. Though the room was lit up with bright fluorescent lights, there was a sense of darkness that came over me, much like the lack of light I saw in the eyes of the people committed to the hospital. There was an unspoken pain buried deep inside, a deep yearning to be free. I could also sense suffering, that there were wounds that needed to be healed. Addiction had really stolen their inner life force and spirits away.

I've never been able to fully escape the memory of what I saw during that visit. As the owner of the facility, Dr Hutaisot, guided me and explained how addiction could really cause serious mental illness, the more this experience haunted me. 'Brain function diminishes as their level of addiction increases,' he said. 'And of course, along with the kind of drugs they are addicted to, the chance to a full recovery is slim to none. But I believe in miracles, because I have seen one or two cases where these kids were totally cured overnight, literally.' *What a life wasted*, I thought to myself. *They are so young yet trapped in the empty shell of addiction. Miracles? Yes, I believe in them too but why gamble on it?*

That day was the first time I visited a mental institution. Witnessing the destruction of drug abuse gave another edge to my whole experience. My heart was really crushed to see these young lives broken into pieces. But I really didn't think that I had the capacity to get into clinical treatment. *What can I really do to make things better around here?* I pondered. But at the same time, I was wondering whether there was any way to prevent this addiction in the first place. People say, 'curiosity killed the cat'. In this case, curiosity about drugs kills people, at least the future of these young people. *There must be something that can be done to help these young people resist unhealthy curiosity*, I thought. But I saw no way out then and I was left with little hope.

'Vera, I think you need to meet George Anadorai,' said Pak Sukirno on a fine evening as we locked the office doors behind us. Pak Sukirno Tarjadi was the secretary general of YCAB Foundation at the time. He then continued, 'George spent his life working with and counselling young people and helping rehabilitate them so that they could reintegrate into the community. Many of them were broken by dysfunctional families or had made poor choices, such as experimenting with drugs.'

Hmm, here's another treatment expert, I thought to myself, disagreeing inside. Then Pak Sukirno added, 'Why don't we invite George to speak and train a group of people here in counselling. We can really learn from his vast experience and counselling technique.' I thought it was a good idea. That was something that could benefit YCAB in its service to the schools. A few weeks later, George arrived in Jakarta and there was a class of eager aspiring counsellors waiting to learn from him.

During the training, I could sense George's deep commitment to mending broken lives through counselling. He was indeed someone who had enough exposure in this field to advise me about the suffering of these young lives in depth. He said, 'Now you have probably sensed how addiction destroys lives. And when it comes to addiction, all you can see is pure evil. But we can prevent it. It's possible.' I became immensely interested as he continued, 'There are ways to prevent this brokenness in young lives. The best way is to prevent them from using drugs in the first place. Knowledge is power. They need to know. It is as simple as that.'

So there is hope. It is preventable! Later I learned that 'primary prevention' was the official term for this type of preventative activity. It is the prevention of drug experimentation in the first place, way before addiction comes into play. It was health education! I was sold right away. George convinced me that preventative methods – albeit difficult to measure – were desperately needed by our young people. *They need to know.*

They need the information before it is too late. What a powerful statement! Young people can be taught to make smart decisions. They need to be given the opportunity to understand about the danger of experimenting with and abusing drugs. They need to understand that the harm that drugs do to the brain is irreversible. Those statements just stuck in my mind.

Intrigued by the potential of prevention education, I later learned that there were a couple of prevention education studies published in Thailand and Australia. 'Something worth learning,' George said when he suggested I take a learning journey to those countries to really understand the kind of prevention programmes they have and how they are run. Most importantly, I wanted to know how the success rate of these programmes was measured and what the key indicators of success were in preventing risky decisions. The main point being that it is possible to prevent risky behaviour and that was enough to propel me to do something, leaving me hopeful.

During my learning journey, I learned that it was all about formulating the right educational approach in disseminating information about the dangers of drug abuse to the children who would otherwise be reckless about the use of drugs or risky behaviour in general. This included training the children to make smart decisions in their lives and how to cope with peer pressure. In the months following the trip, we found ourselves formulating our own ways of addressing teens' risky behaviour. From there onwards, YCAB's first pillar, HeLP (Healthy Lifestyle Promotion) was born in November 1999.

Our programme is simple. We provide education about healthy

lifestyle and life skills training in schools, targeting youths mainly between the ages of fourteen and eighteen. The idea is to help youth to grow their self worth and self confidence in handling social situations in which peer pressure is prevalent. That was the first year when we brought this health education programme to around 2,000 teenagers. Eighteen years down the line, we have reached out to 3.24 million teenagers. And the outcome of our programme has been quite promising. The effectiveness of the programme is measured through pre- and post-tests in which we find significant difference, a good 'delta' as we call it. We have seen an increase in knowledge and a convincing shift in the intention of youths to experiment in risky behaviour, in this case drug abuse and irresponsible sex. The change of behaviour in primary prevention programmes is known to be difficult to measure unless one can find a representative size of an isolated control.

Decades into running the HeLP programme, there are two things I have realised. First, I finally feel like I have responded well to the queries and anxieties of many young parents of my generation. I have helped to address the fears they have about the worst things that could happen to their children. The very least we can do is to prevent the brain damage caused by substance abuse which could cause them to become like the unwanted babies of Kolkata.

I am very pleased to learn that there are ways to prevent our children from engaging in risky behaviour. It was important for me, too, as by then I already had Phil and Adelle. I am also convinced that information is power. The right information given at the right time can move the hearts of young people and protect them from any meaningless and unhealthy decisions they might make to 'play with fire', fire that comes with a lifetime of consequence of addiction or brokenness. That is the most important thing: every parent needs be the primary source of information for his or her children.

The second thing I learned was that addressing risky behaviour requires a holistic approach. Interactive education and training as well as empowering youth with knowledge and life skills is one thing, but if we fail to address the underlying issues, despite knowing the real danger of engaging in risky behaviour, we will never make a difference.

Only years later I learned that there was one root cause to most risky behaviour: vulnerability. There are two powerful Bahasa words: *kemiskinan* and *kebodohan*, which respectively mean poverty and ignorance. Surely, a lack of education makes young people dangerously vulnerable. However, economic deprivation can also bring a worse kind of vulnerability. The reality is 2 million youths drop out of high school every year in Indonesia, mostly due to economic reasons. Even if school tuition is made free, going to school at the very least will incur transport costs and the need for lunch money. No school and no education means no future. Vulnerability is what we fight against. The answer to vulnerability is empowerment.

That's what led YCAB into the youth empowerment space. We do this by giving dropouts and impoverished youth hope and opportunities through education and economic empowerment. During the years of my long learning journey I have realised that these two aspects have to be addressed hand-in-hand in order to create a sustainable change.

My mind kept going back to the double-disabled children in Kolkata. Sometimes it can seem more painful for us to bear witness to their disabilities than it is for them to live with them. Simply because they're born that way and have learned to cope and adjust, they know no other way of living. Amazingly, some of them can be as inspiring as motivational speaker Nick Vujicic who was born without arms and legs and authored *Life Without Limits*. Nick refused to be depressed or negative; instead he chose to be positive. He shares this positivity with millions of others by telling his story at motivational speaking engagements and in his book.

Kemiskinan and *kebodohan* are like double disabilities that can prevent society from progressing. The big question is how can we make people want to progress? How can we inspire them to fight for better lives? How can we make the 'double-disabled' members of our society – the poor and the uneducated – fight like Nick and become inspirational like him?

YCAB's work means nothing if the subjects of our empowerment do not want to progress as much as we want them to. There needs to be mutual understanding and cooperation to make things work. Sometimes they want progress but their ecosystem isn't supportive of it. This lack of support can be both internal and external. Internal factors include mindset and a crippled spirit i.e. lack of fighting spirit; external factors can be family, friends, or the community around them. Below is one example in which we experienced an unsupportive external factor (the school) that impeded us from reaching out to our beneficiaries, the students.

The incident occurred during the early years of our school-to-school programme. This was when we had just begun our healthy lifestyle campaign. Back then I was pretty naïve. I thought that if we gave our best to do good, everyone would accept us with open arms. However, to my dismay, programmes that we offered free of charge to the schools – which could potentially benefit their students – were not always accepted. It was during this time that I was introduced to the real paradox of giving. I received suspicion and scepticism in return for my intention to do good.

Some schools suspected us of having ulterior motives. They thought we had built aspects into the programme that would mean needing to purchase other services from us. Some wanted us to simply pay them. Apparently there was an unspoken cost per student we needed to pay them to let us train their students. The 'costs' were usually the budget we needed to give for the school to buy food or to set up the room for the programme. If the school could make a profit, they would happily open their doors and accept our programme. But I chose not to give in to their system of values. It was indeed hard to shake off the bitter feeling and distrust. It almost made me want to give up.

I had no choice but to fight back and endure. I knew I would find a way to turn the tide of this suspicion. People have simply lost hope. They have no hope for the goodness that people can do for each other. No one could believe that we wanted to come to them and offer free programmes without any benefit to ourselves. The only way to move forward was to negotiate with them without compromising our values. Later I learned that giving the schools all the credit for our programmes' success was the only effective solution. Schools can earn brownie points from the government, and that's something of which they can be proud. We tweaked the approach and finally came up with a win-win solution without compromising our values and YCAB's policy.

This was an induction period for YCAB. It was a steep learning curve we experienced as we created our first pillar. I had to bear this reality of navigating our programme, until one day, in early April 2000, I got the chance to meet with the Minister of Education, Yahya Muhaimin. In my meeting with him, I shared my heartache. Like a daughter confiding to her father, I poured out my disappointment about the system to him. Pak Yahya was gracious in listening to my frustrations and he empathised with me. I was there with a couple of board members, and after listening intently to what I had to say, Pak Yahya finally responded, 'Okay, so why don't I write you a recommendation letter?' He called his secretary in and briefed him about the letter.

That afternoon I walked out of the Minister's office holding in my hand a recommendation letter that forever changed YCAB's future. I think perhaps the secretary to the Minister prepared the letter in a rush, because it didn't have an expiry date. It basically endorsed YCAB to go to schools and all education offices under the Minister of Education of Indonesia. Schools were requested to give their full support to YCAB's healthy lifestyle and drug prevention programmes. At that time, everything was centralised, so that recommendation letter was faxed through to all the education offices across all the provinces in Indonesia, including to some parts of Indonesia that were otherwise unreachable. To our surprise, it was a very powerful letter! It truly turned the tide for the HeLP programme.

A few months after the meeting with the Minister we launched our first education tour from Java to Bali. I couldn't believe how many doors the Minister's letter opened, doors that otherwise would have remained firmly closed. 'Oh, is this YCAB? We got the letter from the Minister recommending your foundation to our school!' The meeting with the Minister was our second most important divine intervention, after the UN Award. It was a fast track that has enabled YCAB to reach millions of young people. All it took was that one gracious meeting with the Minister. God moved him to have so much faith in us, and the rest is history.

Doing good is good, but not enough. How can anyone who wants to make a difference in Indonesia do it without being hobbled? What would have happened if I didn't have a link to this kind Minister? I knew it could've been the end of everything. A part of my heart was torn apart, a part of me almost died. It was like a double-edged sword; I almost got emotionally wounded while trying to cure the world around me of *kemiskinan* and *kebodohan*. But God came to my rescue and whispered to my heart, 'Not yet, Vera. I will make a way where you don't see a way. I will make a way for you to pass through the wilderness.'

※ ※ ※

'I am the person in charge here, and for the kind of work we've done, this is certainly not enough!' screamed the boy in front of us while slamming down the IDR10,000 bill Pieter had given him. Apparently, the last in line was the head of the gang and he thought that the incentive to clean their own place was not enough. I panicked. Prince Albert had just arrived near the coast of Sirombu while I was screaming inside, *What are we doing still dealing with these ungrateful little thugs? Why are we entertaining their nasty attitude? Why are we paying them anything to clean their own space?*

I decided to walk away, I just did not know how to react. I thought Pieter would be able to deal with them, because I couldn't. I was furious. And the whole team was, too. We were dismayed by the reaction of these people who had received new land, new housing, new schools as well as a community centre. We had worked so hard to make sure that the reconstruction project ensured the highest quality of life for the tsunami victims and their families. Their ungratefulness was heartbreaking and it caused pain that I had never experienced before. I couldn't put it into words. After all we had given them, they were asking for a broom to sweep their floors with. 'You gave us everything but the broom to keep the house clean like you want it.' *Like we want? Really! It is their house, their life. All we ask is to keep it clean for half a day in exchange for tens of thousands of dollars' worth of new property. I guess it is too much to ask.*

I stepped away and followed the welcoming committee to greet Prince Albert. From a distance, I saw the Prince disembark from the yacht onto a smaller boat before coming ashore. As I watched him wave at the little welcoming committee, I felt so honoured to be there to receive him alongside our partners. *Here is the Prince I have only ever seen in magazines or tabloids. He has come all the way from Monaco to officiate the opening of a housing facility that will house more than 250 families stricken by the tsunami. I need to imprint this scene in my memory, this is something I want to remember all my life.*

Yet deep inside, I was still digesting what happened earlier when the youngsters of the village had demanded more money. I remembered what's written in the book of Mark, chapter 12, verse 41–44:

Jesus sat down opposite the place where the offerings were put and watched the crowd putting their money into the temple treasury. Many rich people threw in large amounts. But a poor widow came and put in two very small copper coins, worth only a few cents. Calling his disciples to him, Jesus said, 'Truly I tell you, this poor widow has put more into the treasury than all the others. They all gave out of their wealth; but she, out of her poverty, put in everything – all she had to live on.'

As I thought about the story of the widow's offering, and how she – out of all people – had given the most, simply because she had given out of her poverty. She had given more than she could spare. Then I recalled the wooden sign that I had seen on the wall at the Mother House in Kolkata that said 'Give, but give until it hurts'. It was then that I began to see the beauty of experiencing pain in giving. This is a God-given opportunity for the haves to enjoy the bliss of giving. Otherwise, how else could the haves, those who have more than this poor widow, ever give sacrificially when they give from abundance? Surely, Jesus is not excluding wealthy people from doing good by being generous with their money. Surely, the haves can touch God's heart too with their giving. But how? How can they ever give 'out of their poverty'?

It is true that to give with meaning is to give with the right motive. In many cases, unless people give more than they can afford to give, the feeling of sacrifice seems a little distant. I know of a few wealthy people who do, like the Colgate family or even Bill Gates, but how many really would? How can the wealthy ever give 'out of their poverty' without giving the majority of their worth? Could it be, the emotional pain that I suffered when faced with the ingratitude of the tsunami survivors is the pain, the hurt, that Jesus referred to? Can the type of pain that you feel when you give without getting thanks in return – or are criticised for the way that you give – become the sacrificial part, the 'poverty' part which equals the 'giving everything you have to live on' part of the verse?

It was an epiphany. I finally understood that giving is a vertical business. It is a part of acting out our love for God in our deep personal relationship with Him. It doesn't matter if people reject you and seem ungrateful for what you've done, or whether the recipients are scolding you for the way that you give. This may come as a surprise, but it's true. It was something that YCAB had experienced before. We once received a very special teaching moment when we were scolded for giving *too much* rice. It happened during our annual staple food distribution in commemoration of Indonesia's independence day. We usually give basic food to the poor in the community we serve, and we wanted to give as much rice as we could. So we distributed one package per family consisting of a twenty-five-kilogram bag of rice, a bag of cooking oil and a bag of sugar. However, many were happy, but also a bit unimpressed. A very mixed emotion indeed.

Some of them complained that twenty-five kilos of rice was too much to carry. Couldn't YCAB have given them ten or fifteen kilograms instead? A smaller bag would be easier to carry and they wouldn't have to pay for transport to get it home. As givers, we learnt something that day. We learnt how to give wisely, not too much, not too little.

This incident really taught me that when you give, it is between you and God alone. I understand now that this is how wealthy people can still give 'out of their poverty', how they can give with a sacrificial heart. It does not depend on the amount of money they give: the sacrificial giving comes from the heart. They may have demotivating experiences but they have to continue to give nevertheless.

On the contrary, if someone gives out of pride or a desire to be seen and praised, even though they keep on giving and it may please the recipients of their charity, it doesn't really impact their heavenly treasure. So when wealthy people give out of a sacrificial heart and experience a kind of pain in whatever form, it is a good thing. I believe that through it, they qualify as the kind of givers that touch God's heart.

I see this as the integration of my work life and faith. We can't compartmentalise how we work, how we live with our family, and how we serve at church. Our whole life is an act of worship. Our whole life must be presented as a living sacrifice. That is how worship became very personal to me. It is to continue living while sacrificing many aspects of my life, including welcoming all the pains, and accepting them as part of giving.

But aside from the sacrificial element of giving, I was also reminded of another element of giving: being a cheerful giver. God loves a cheerful giver. So how do we integrate the two, pain and cheerfulness? How can the pain from giving sacrificially coexist with giving with a cheerful heart? It sounds contradictory to me, but being full of cheer while experiencing pain is possible. Sirombu taught me this.

After the official ceremony, the Prince's inspection found the community centre spotless. The day was finally won. Prince Albert was impressed with the buildings and the houses, and I was so glad his presence could turn hostility into hospitality.

One thing that I cannot forget is something that he said to me, as if he knew what we had been through that morning. 'At the end of the day, Vera, it is not about providing them with houses,' he paused and looked me in the eyes before he continued. 'It is about giving them hope.' I was struck by his remark. 'Hope that the outside world cares for them. Hope is what moves them and therefore changes them. Hope is a powerful tool for survival.' I nodded my agreement, speechless, while slowly digesting his wisdom about hope.

I wondered what made him say this, exactly when I needed to hear it. A verse came flashing through my mind. *And now these three remain: faith, hope, and love. But the greatest of these is love.*

Aha, love! There I came to truly understand that it is the vertical relationship to God that demands us to love horizontally, love our fellow men. Love can turn hostility into hospitality, I witnessed just that in Sirombu. Love gave the disabled and unwanted children of Kolkata reasons to live in spite of all their adversity. Love made me go on, it reaffirmed my calling. Love inspired me to launch YCAB. Love enabled the widow in the parable to give everything she had. If she could, why can't we?

Eventually, love conquers all. Love enables giving. Love is powerful. Love God, love the world, that's the pure principle of giving and why we give. Through faith, YCAB continued to go from school to school despite the early rejection and we continued to hope that one day the schools would see the benefit of our programme. We relentlessly showed our love to the people of Sirombu, and the best part of it was we gave and we learned not to expect anything back from them.

Perfect, thank you God! What a great opportunity to learn the true lesson of giving. To give out of our own poverty: to be cheerful even when our giving causes us emotional pain or trauma. Give until it hurts.

After we left that day, hope was the one thing they had in Sirombu. Hope is all I have too as I continue to grow YCAB. We continue to extend goodness to places where our programme is welcomed and appreciated at face value.

'Taking action, getting our hands dirty, is the only way we can achieve our life's mission, fulfilling the meaning of our existence in this life. That's what truly matters.'

chapter

LEADING CHANGE: THE FOUR SEASONS

'Life Is Beautiful In His Wonderful Time'

I believe that life is as much about the journey as it is about the destination. It is about the warmth of the summer that keeps us hopeful throughout the beautiful falling leaves in autumn and into the freezing cold of winter, which then transitions into the simple blossoming miracle of spring. Suffering is a temporary thing, and hope is always just around the corner because after winter must come spring.

※ ※ ※

'Remember, Mum? That New Year's Eve in London, when the snow started to fall right after the stroke of midnight?' Joey's eyes fill with excitement as he continues to reminisce. 'We thought it must have been part of the show, but it was not!' That was the last time we had experienced a snowy winter. And it was almost seven years ago. He is right, it was magical how the snow had begun to fall at the stroke of midnight, marking the birth of 2010. His eyes light up brightly as he retells the story, as bright as the sunlight reflected off the powdery snow in Aomori, Japan where we are travelling. His cheeks are flushed with the cold as he speaks of how much he misses skiing, partly blaming me, Philmon and Adelle because we all have suffered significant injuries, making us reluctant to partake in more physically demanding activities and sports.

Again Joey is right. We are scared of going through the pain and rehabilitation of more injuries, and so our holidays are less sporty than they used to be. However, on this vacation Joey will have the opportunity to ski again and his joyful expression and excited energy is contagious. It wipes out the fatigue from the eight-hour flight and an hour on the snowy road. The time we spend with loved ones is the most precious time. It is that thought that helps recharge my energy.

The ski resort that we are travelling to is owned by one of Pieter's colleagues and is located in Aomori, across the Tsugaru Strait from Hokkaido. It sits on 120 hectares, and is home to three ski resorts, five ski lifts, and a golf course in the summer. As we settle in on our first night, Joey is extremely excited that he is going to be able to ski tomorrow. We have brought all our ski gear with us, but Joey has grown so much since we last skied that he doesn't even fit into his big brother's old gear. Time to shop! Luckily there is a little ski shop in the hotel lobby. From its limited selection Joey manages to gather everything he needs for the trip.

After our mini shopping expedition, I set up my laptop in our room and realise the *fubuki* – the whirling snowstorm whipped up by the wind – outside the window is biting cold and quite intense. I have never seen such eerily captivating lashing winds and dancing snow. The coldness is ferociously enchanting in a way that is hard to describe.

The bewitching mood of the enigmatic weather reminds me of the 'coldness' that YCAB had experienced in its growth as a social enterprise. I still remember how naïve we were when we began our journey eighteen years ago in 1999. We didn't know we were building a social enterprise; we didn't even know what a social enterprise was. All we knew was we wanted to create a foundation and we needed to set up a few companies to help keep it afloat. That's the sustainability angle that for me has been and always will be first and foremost. Running programmes always requires money, therefore income-generating activities should be a top priority for an organisation that calls itself a social enterprise.

Each of our programmes was born out of need and was relatively organic in its inception. As time passed, we found ourselves running the three pillars of health promotion (HeLP), education for the poor (HoLD) and economic empowerment (HOpE). Over time, I feel there has been a bit of disintegration.

At best a segregation that divides them; at worst a total disconnection. Between the three, HeLP became somewhat mutually exclusive from HoLD and HOpE.

Historically, YCAB is known for its school campaign programme called HeLP (an abbreviation of Healthy Lifestyle Programme) that was created in 1999. This programme provides soft-skills and life-skills training to more than 100,000 youth every year. This training is aimed at equipping students to embrace a healthy lifestyle; it educates them about drug abuse, reproductive and sexual health, and how to handle relationship problems such as conflict resolution and bullying. Then a few years later, HoLD – an abbreviation for House of Learning and Development (also known as Rumah Belajar in Bahasa) – was launched. HoLD provides education, including vocational skills, for low-income youth and school dropouts. Paired with the economic empowerment programme that touches both the youth, by offering jobs after graduation, and their mothers, by giving them access to capital or microloans through our microfinance programme, HOpE (Hands-on Operation for Entrepreneurship) completes what HoLD begins.

We have learned that if we want to help alleviate poverty, education is pivotal. Education can break the poverty cycle. However, education and economic empowerment cannot be addressed in isolation; each interchangeably affects the success of the other. We are mindful that parents can sometimes be reluctant to support their children in going back to school because it means the children will have less time to help make money for the family. Replacing the income that is earned by the children is thus seen as very important in order for parents to allow their children to further their education.

So by making the continued education of the children of our borrowers a prerequisite for a loan, we are, in fact, addressing the school dropout situation. YCAB's microfinance helps achieve the ultimate goal: education for all. This makes our microfinance very different from mainstream microfinance. Our microfinance is very mission-driven; it is used as the means to an end, with the ultimate mission being *kemandirian* ('independence' or 'self-reliance').

We believe education is good, but it's not enough. We cannot just stop there. We need to help the young people find jobs once they have completed their education. That's what makes true independence possible. I learned this in my journey growing YCAB: education and economic empowerment need to be addressed simultaneously. And we can only know that from listening to the needs of our beneficiaries, hence the birth of our education-linked microfinance in 2010.

However, there's an incomplete aspect to YCAB's work. We need to integrate the three pillars, and the journey to do so feels like a long and winding road that YCAB has to travel. It's a journey into the unknown, and the idea of it chills my bones. There's a cold isolation in trying to bring the three pillars together. It has been a long dreadful winter for YCAB.

I think it is part of life's process to break down in the coldness of winter before blossoming in the springtime. It is simply how nature works; it is a natural process. Like other things in life, in order to build something, sometimes one must have the courage to tear something else down. I have a feeling that we need to first diffuse HeLP in order to infuse it into HoLD and HOpE.

In addition to this, we also face another kind of *fubuki* or storm – it is in the form of the unpredictability of financial sustainability. While we do earn money through our business units, the social outreach costs more than what they bring in. Time is what we need. In order to achieve 100 per cent sustainability, our business units need to grow to a certain size. The problem is that, companies don't break even overnight. Most of them do not actually earn money in their first year or two. Others take years to mature. Everything has its own process, and everything has to go through its own seasons, struggling through the cold winter and then blossoming in the spring.

So there are two core concepts that need to be considered: sustainability and integration. Unlike the *fubuki* of integration, I think that our sustainability trajectory is moving so much faster towards spring. With the promising business model that grew out of my duty to chaperone Adelle during a project for school in which she learnt how microfinancing was utilised by banks and non-financial institutions, the future is looking brighter. The projection clearly shows that if microfinance reaches three or four times its current amount, we will be able to maintain 100 per cent of our programmes.

With that hope, the summer of sustainability is really coming. I can already feel the warmth of the sunshine on my face. However, these two aspects are not the only ones that bring the chill of winter to my journey. Paving a new way, whether personal or organisational, takes a lot of faith and courage. I need courage to keep walking down this cold, dark alley with a lantern in my hand. I need faith to take each step down the limited path lit up by the lantern.

※ ※ ※

The *fubuki* is still whirling outside as we get ready to sleep. The whirling snow makes me wonder if it will be safe for Joey to ski the next day. I can't even guess at what his reaction will be if I try to forbid it. I can't bear to break his heart when he is so close to fulfilling his desire to ski again. I have to take a step of faith and believe that Joey will make the right and safe decision.

Faith is a gift. It is so easy to say we have faith, but our faith in the light at the end of the tunnel is tested on a daily basis. When it comes to faith, there are good and bad days: good when we are optimistic, bad when we are doubtful. But as a leader I must be in control – doubt is something I have to try not to show. In situations when others doubt, leaders are supposed to show strength and determination. Many times YCAB's then chief of finance, Lanny Halim, and chief of administration, Moni Rejeki, came to me anxious and concerned about whether we had enough cash flow to survive another quarter. And usually, after they shared their concerns with me, I would say, 'We will do what we need to do to survive, but please have faith. All of our needs will be provided for.' And for eighteen years, we have been blessed with sufficiency. Many times it has seemed to us that it has been divine intervention that has made our survival possible. It is simply the journey of *ora et labora* – pray hard and work hard. I believe that we must strive to do our best, but doing it with full knowledge that there are times when we need to know when to stop and allow a greater power than ourselves – God – to do the rest.

I see more value in striving than worrying. Worrying really changes nothing. Worry introduces unnecessary negative energy into our surroundings. Being discouraged gets us nowhere. And when leading an organisation – especially a non-profit social enterprise like YCAB – a leader's strength is needed to rise above difficult times.

※ ※ ※

'Good night, Mum,' Joey says and gives me a long, tight hug. I think about how blissful moments often involve both joy and anxiety as I watch Joey close his bedroom door.

Joy and anxiety are the two things that colour my journey with YCAB. My joy is complete when I see one impoverished youth continue his or her education and go on to earn a livelihood. His or her life is changed and he or she is transformed from a scavenger, domestic helper or dropout into a productive young member of society who has skills and is able to hold down a job. My anxiety comes when I am faced with the question of YCAB's survival and impact. How can we secure funding for almost 800 employees and, at the programme level, how can we ensure that each youth we educate can become *mandiri* – self-reliant – through jobs or the micro businesses they develop with our seed capital. To us, that's the real impact of everything we do.

Anxiety is a funny thing. Funny because it has both negative and positive sides. The negative can provoke the positive in a good way; for example, our worry makes us work harder. There have been shades of anxiety at every stage of YCAB's growth. In the beginning we didn't know how we could survive, now we need to worry about how we can create lasting impact and sustain our current position, e.g. in the global ranking of NGOs. Every year before the ranking is released, I am anxious about our position. Have we held firm, moved up, or moved down? YCAB is currently the only Indonesian NGO ranked among the Top 100 NGOs. We come in at number forty, after having moved steadily up from seventy-four to sixty-three to forty-nine to forty-four. To maintain our upward trajectory we need to maintain our presence; presence can be gained by showing evidence of impact.

Sometimes I wonder why I am so ambitious. Why do I feel driven to reach out to millions of youth through YCAB? Why am I so obsessed in leading that change? Why do I feel as though YCAB will be my enduring legacy, the mark I leave on the world? So now my anxiety moves beyond survival and sustainability to legacy.

I believe it all goes back to why YCAB was born. It was born out of my spiritual journey to make sense of my life. There was a sense of urgency to optimise my God-given talents and a sense of responsibility to mark my existence in this world. I have always had an unwavering ambition to be remembered as more than a mother and wife.

I have always believed that I was made for a purpose greater than myself. I have lived my life in such a way to prepare for something big. I don't know why I feel a calling to serve the poor, while my peers work on developing their careers. I don't have the answer as to why I am so different. It is important to know that not even once have I ever considered myself superior to anyone else because I have chosen to help others.

All professions have dignity and everyone should consider what they do as part of worship. Therefore, whatever their job is, a spiritual person does it in service to the real big boss, God, and not to their human boss. That's why I feel so very blessed to be able to give the best part of my life to contribute to the world around me. I consider it a true privilege to serve the poor.

The guiding principles and the built-in values that I believe in are the very premise of leadership, something I learned at the Kennedy School at Harvard University. Bill George, a professor at the Harvard Business School, teaches people to reach down and search their lives. We must embrace all the pain and joy, all the experiences to which we are exposed: all the experiences in our lives that make us, us – every high, every low, every drip and scrap of it. Our experiences make us an 'authentic' person. Only an authentic person can be an authentic leader. But that's not enough. An authentic leader has to have a guiding light in their life, a True North, which is the title of Bill's book.

True North explains that a person's values act as the framework for his or her life. Values, when paired with authenticity, can lead to good and lasting leadership. And that's exactly what people want to see and feel. People want to see leaders with values and they want to feel their sincerity. Leaders who have gone through good and bad in life, yet persistently continue to thrive; nothing can stop them from realising their vision. People also want to see both the strengths and the weaknesses of their leaders; it helps them understand that leaders are human: they have suffered setbacks like everyone else, yet they have managed to prevail. People want to feel the passion of their leaders, so they can choose whether to follow or not follow, to subscribe or not to subscribe to their leader's missions.

Passion is a powerful thing, but it has to be guided by a certain set of values so that you can be the authentic leader that people want to follow. People need to believe in your passion and your values in order to voluntarily trace your footsteps. The keyword here is 'voluntarily'; it makes all the difference when people follow their leaders because they are willing, not because they must. That's real power.

That's how Bill George affected me. I have come to understand that a good leader is an authentic one. Being authentic is being at peace with ourselves, who we are and where we come from. That means we must accept everything about us, embracing all the bad and the good. We must accept all that has happened in the past, all the experiences and learning, even character faults, our strength and failures. We've got to own them all. Most importantly, Bill underlines the importance of being guided by a set of values and a calling. Real leaders are authentic because they are inflamed by a real passion to create change.

What impressed me most about Bill was his humility and gracefulness in teaching the class. That is what really won me over. It was the inaugural global leadership class that I participated in as the newly appointed Young Global Leader of the World Economic Forum in 2009. Bill taught me what authentic leadership looks like, and how we can become leaders as long as we stay true to ourselves, uphold our values and, of course, understand our true calling.

The calling part is the most difficult part to explain. Of course, a calling has to be something that moves us, something that really disrupts our peace and makes us want to do something about it. I was reassured about the concept of a calling when I attended another leadership programme at MIT. In the *Theory U: Leading from the Future as it Emerges*, Otto Scharmer identifies dynamic leaders as those who are constantly learning and reflecting. They should embrace and master the two learning cycles: one, learning by reflecting on the experiences of the past; two, learning from the future as it emerges (*presencing*).

Leaders, Scharmer stresses, must be able to 'connect to the Inner Source' in order to be at the state of 'presencing'. Presencing is an amalgam of 'presence' and 'sensing'. It means that it is imperative for leaders to be mindful of their surroundings – that's what being present and relevant is all about. Then, Scharmer continues to say that the quality of attention and intention of a leader is what determines their leadership quality.

But what exactly does connecting to one's Inner Source mean? To me it sounds like listening to one's inner voice. But since Scharmer capitalises 'Inner Source', it seems to me that the inner voice is not just our own voice. It's something more transcendental. Although it is never explicitly stated, I think Scharmer equates the Inner Source to a divine entity.

I personally see this Inner Source as God. As a Christian,

I believe that God lives within us through His spirit. He is the ultimate 'True North', the Giver of our values and moral framework in life. He is the one who guides and leads us to our own individual calling and spiritual journey, and sets the very purpose of our life for His glory.

Looking at things through these three lenses – practical, academic and spiritual – I have to come to uniquely understand that the spiritual quality of a leader determines the quality of their leadership. It is the interior condition of oneself that brings out the supremacy of one's leadership. Our hearts need to be sincerely open and mindful, sensitive to a calling and open to a vision. And we can only achieve this by submitting ourselves to the Inner Source – which is God for believers.

Submission is one thing, but there should be something that comes out of it. According to Scharmer, and something which I myself have also experienced, it is imperative to have the willingness to do something that links our hearts, head and hands together. This is to rise up and attempt to, in his words, 'co-create a prototype of the new' approach for change, and to keep on growing it as we go on perfecting this 'the new' thing until the desired transformation is achieved.

Taking action, getting our hands dirty, is the only way we can achieve our life's mission, fulfilling the meaning of our existence in this life. That's what truly matters. And I find both Scharmer and Bill George to be quite consistent in their leadership proposition. And isn't it fascinating to learn how these two academic giants carefully chose secular words to describe what I interpret as the spiritual realm?

When I experienced my own calling in 1998, it was a very spiritual experience. I believe I was responding to God's prompting and decided to take action to respond to the questions that kept pounding in my heart and my mind: *How do I want to be remembered? What is the meaning and purpose of my life? What kind of legacy will I leave behind?*

Eighteen months later, on 13 August 1999, I responded to my calling by signing a notarial decree number thirteen establishing YCAB in Jakarta. That was where we began the journey to lead change in the lives of marginalised youth.

But why did those questions matter to me? I know now that it was my spirituality – the connection with my God – that was, and remains, the source of it. Complemented by the perspectives I gained from Bill George and Otto Scharmer, I am fully aware now that my leadership journey is pretty much identical to my spiritual journey. For some time I had thought that YCAB was *the product* of my spiritual journey. In fact, leading YCAB *is* my spiritual journey.

As the years pass, my spiritual journey has continued. It has taken me slowly but surely from a calling to an ambition. This happened when I became aware of the scope of the needs of Indonesia's youth. Simply put, growth becomes necessary so that I can stay faithful to my calling: to reach the millions of underprivileged youth in Indonesia. My calling demands that we evolve, that we grow from good to great.

Doing things well and to be great at what we do requires a submissive heart. If your heart is in the right place, your passion is felt and people will follow you out of love, and not fear. That's what true leadership is all about.

※ ※ ※

After three full days of fun and memorable skiing, Joey is sad to say goodbye to the powdery snow of Aomori and the new friends he has made, friends who helped him improve his skills and taught him some new tricks.

'Have you seen Joey?' I ask Pieter, two hours before we are supposed to leave for Tokyo. 'He should be back now for his lunch.' My anxiety continues to escalate when some of the other skiers return and ask me where Joey has been all morning. I thought he was with them out on the slopes.

I begin to panic. What if he's stranded in the mountains somewhere? Why hasn't he been skiing with the group? Skiing alone is dangerous. My mind races trying to think of an explanation as to where Joey can be, while simultaneously figuring out how we can still get to Tokyo if we miss our flight. As I discuss our options with a member of hotel staff, a skier drops in and tells me he has just seen Joey rushing back to his room, apparently he lost track of the time. I am so relieved. At least my Joey is not lost.

A few hours later Pieter, Joey and I arrive in Tokyo. Phil and Adelle are scheduled to meet us there the next day. We are excited to be in Tokyo, not least for the great food it has to offer. The food at the ski resort was great, but the selection was limited and the nearest restaurants were at least ten to fifteen miles away in the snow. In Tokyo there is great food everywhere you look.

The next morning I am awakened by voices outside my bedroom. Even though it's very early in the morning, I get up. 'Hi Mum. We're here!' Adelle greets me. As Phil hugs me he says, 'Sorry, we didn't mean to wake you up. But now that you're up, do you want to have breakfast?' I nod in response. He smiles and starts to order room service.

Ever since she was small, Adelle has been our family's master holiday planner. I can see her notes all over the coffee table. She has written down travel plans for the next four days we are going to spend in Tokyo. She has listed which restaurants to visit, things to eat, must-try ice cream, and the best *matcha* in town. I still have some of the travel scribbles she made when she was six. The only thing that has changed since then is that now she mostly makes her notes on her phone, not on paper.

One of the must-try places she has noted is a small restaurant called Makoto. We find it later that night located down a very narrow alleyway. It's a humble local place that seats only eight to ten guests. We enjoy some authentic Japanese food and love watching how the chef meticulously prepares each dish with the freshest seasonal ingredients.

YCAB has gone through many seasons during its existence. It seems as though a sprinkle of little miracles here and there has cleared its path so that it could fully bloom into the YCAB of today. From the Minister of Education giving us a national recommendation letter without an expiry date, to gaining recognition from the United Nations, YCAB has been blessed along the way. Sometimes it has been as simple as making small talk with a stranger; a conversation can turn into a new friendship. The interesting part is this: people with different sets of skills and experiences have made their appearance just as YCAB has needed them.

For example, between 2006 and 2009 I started to feel a jolt in my stomach. I felt as if YCAB had all the right ingredients on the table but we didn't know what to cook. We were missing a chef. We needed a chef to figure out the best dish to prepare with the ingredients we had. Then we needed the chef to cook the dish.

The 'ingredients' at hand were our great and passionate people, the YCAB team, the potential of our three programmes and the impact we had the potential to make. The 'dish' that was lacking was a business model, the kind that could secure YCAB's future and ensure its sustainability.

That's when Joe Hsueh showed up. Joe was my MIT leadership classmate in 2009. I remember that a casual chat during a coffee break turned into an interesting discussion about how we could practically implement what we were learning in class. I learnt that he was also a team member of Peter Sengeh's System Dynamic team, and I was fascinated to hear what he had to say about their design approach.

A few months later, Joe visited YCAB in Jakarta and quizzed us for three days, trying to draw out what everybody thought YCAB was all about. The output was phenomenal. Together, we created the closed-loop model. And for the first time, we could see how our three programmes could merge and be drawn into what is now known as YCAB's very own, very first Change Model – which includes and explains the business model towards YCAB's sustainability. We were so thrilled to have that model.

(See chapter four for more detail on the model.)

It's still rough around the edges, but we continue to work on it even today. Such work means it is continually evolving, but nonetheless it makes us more confident. Our dynamic exercise really helps us make more sense of what we're doing in one quick look. The diagram really helps and I feel like we're moving from the coldness of winter into the warmth of spring.

Joe was perhaps YCAB's first chef. Since then there have been more chefs who have helped YCAB, and they all have different backgrounds. Most of them have been big names in consultancy and service providers.

This makes me think of mid-2011, when Boston Consulting Group (BCG) offered us their services pro bono. This was beyond my wildest dreams. BCG found YCAB, a non-profit, and offered their services at no cost? It's almost unheard of. We took this opportunity and we asked them to help us integrate the three programmes – HeLP, HoLD and HOpE – into what we call a Centre of Change, which is designed to have income-generating activity that sustains it. Its implementation is still pending, but I know it will one day come to a close when everything else is ready. 'Everything else' here refers to some processes such as restructuring, system building and change management including expanding all the businesses to support our mission. That has taken – to our surprise – more years than expected to achieve. However, to this day, I don't really know how BCG found us, but they did find us and we are so glad they did. BCG has become YCAB's best friend, and they continue to provide their services.

Changes of season and chefs have been the two things that

keep interchangeably appearing at our door at the right time, offering the right help. It has helped us pave the way to becoming a stronger social enterprise. YCAB's good luck continued when the year after BCG approached us, we found our other best friend, Accenture.

I remember having a brief conversation with a gentleman from Accenture in Davos. There are two kinds of people you meet there: those who say they will follow up on things and don't, and those who say they will and actually do. This fine man was the latter.

After a five- or six-minute exchange during which we each outlined what we do, he wrote an email introducing YCAB to their Indonesian CEO, then Pak Julianto Sidarto. A meeting was set up a few months later, and something just clicked. I told Pak Julianto that we needed Accenture's expertise to help us reach our 2020 vision: to bring YCAB's programmes to 5 million youth in ten countries and to raise USD50 million in social investment funds. In order to reach these goals we needed the appropriate IT infrastructure. It was important to us to build the system so that it was compatible with Microsoft products because they are our official technology partner and they have granted us free access to their licensed products. Creating the IT infrastructure with Accenture has taken quite some time; even now we are still implementing and building the system. But we are incredibly happy that we have a clear way forward for this project.

BCG and Accenture are our chefs numbers two and three. Business model creation and IT infrastructure are now in place. Since then, many others have joined forces to empower YCAB, both consultants or experts and professional volunteers including interns. In addition to BCG and Accenture, we have been so privileged to enjoy years of the commitment of other companies: EY for audit services; Palladium for corporate strategy; PWC for tax; and corporate law firms including AYMP (Indonesia), Holland & Knight and Norton Rose Fulbright (international).

However, there are other invisible hands that have shaped YCAB, the thousands of fine men and women who have volunteered their time and expertise. They are the unsung heroes. They seek no recognition, rather they are simply happy to volunteer their know-how and abilities for the improvement of YCAB. Some will spend only a day at YCAB, while others stay for months. The longest-serving volunteer we had was someone from Singapore Management University (SMU) who stayed for fourteen months. Volunteers from Japan usually stay between six and twelve months. They all work on special projects and assignments to help YCAB's specific needs.

From experts down to interns, we love them all. They all mark their presence uniquely and each leave their own lasting impression. In turn, every time we ask their impression of their time spent at YCAB, almost everyone uses the Bahasa word *kekeluargaan* – a sense of family closeness. It's really heart-warming to know that this is the feeling those who have worked with us side-by-side think of when they think of YCAB. I founded YCAB with the mission that it should spread love to the world, so it is fitting that love is felt internally within the organisation.

Love is a powerful thing. It drives people to give and give. I just cannot imagine how we could go on and expand our work without volunteers, experts and consultants giving us advice on where to go and how to get there. I am forever thankful that guided by these consultants, working pro bono, YCAB is stronger. We have a clearer picture of the terrain ahead, so we can prepare for it while turning something good into better and greater things. It always feels like harvest time is coming. There's an excitement of a bountiful crop. Gradually, we are starting to see a clearer path in front of us, lit up by the golden sun of grace above.

Every step of YCAB's journey thus far has happened in such a way that everything has fallen into place at the perfect time. When Accenture came in to work on project management and change management, transforming YCAB from an implementer to an enabler, it led us onto the path of sustainability. So now that we are set on our programmes, we are trying to increase our financial capability. At the same time, we're trying to wrap ourselves up in one consolidated global vehicle that is known as YCAB Foundation.

The doors that have been opened were opened one by one in the right sequence at the right time, without me even having to fret or plan it. So, I guess throughout all the four seasons, I have learned to let go of control sometimes, to let good things bloom on their own, in their own time.

On the business side, when we started to turn a profit and our business units were able to cover YCAB's administration expenses, we were glowing with hope. It started to feel like all the ingredients were coming together to form a delicious dish. Our hope for total sustainability strengthens each day.

Slowly but surely, our winter has turned into spring and summer, granting YCAB a great feeling of hope. Hope that there will be sunshine throughout the summer, hope that we can achieve integration and sustainability.

The most important thing that I have realised during this journey is that I was never YCAB's head chef. The real head chef is the one with the capital 'C'. The real Chef uses invisible hands that work in and through everyone for the good of YCAB. The missing ingredients, those that were not 'in season', were always provided along the way. Some would call that a miracle. For me, it's simply grace.

※ ※ ※

'Let's say grace for the food,' Pieter says while glancing at Phil as the first dish is presented before us. 'Phil, why don't you lead us in prayer?'

'Thank you God for family time, for bringing us together and for the amazing food we have tonight. We pray for those in need, those in times of trouble; we pray that you will also provide for them. Amen.' Phil closed the prayer, marking the beginning of our family meal.

We went on to enjoy nine dishes that night, *omakase* style. While we thoroughly enjoy the food, the greatest part is the company and the joy of being together.

Life is sometimes served *omakase* style. Tom Hanks as Forrest Gump famously said 'Life is like a box of chocolates, you never know what you're going to get'. Such is *omakase* style, we don't know what the next dish is going to be, but we are happily surprised by each presentation and by the taste of each individual dish.

My life since Harvard has been a kind of *omakase*. I remember my first day at Harvard as a new Young Global Leader (YGL). I didn't know anyone there and was sharing a table with complete strangers. For our first assignment we were divided into small groups of five or six people and we were to meet every morning before the class started and work through Bill George's *True North* workbook.

Working through the exercises together really forced us to open up to the people in our small group. Opening up our hearts, sharing our stories, struggles, successes and failures. Fortunately, my group bonded naturally, while other groups fell apart. They just disintegrated after a few morning meetings and never rebounded. I was so lucky to have been assigned to a group that stayed together. We learnt about each other and supported each other through the exercises.

I remember the first morning my group met. I felt like a fish out of water; everyone else was an inspiring, intelligent young leader, a true pioneer in his or her field. Ellana Lee was a member of my group and she later became one of my dearest friends. Not a day goes by without me thanking God for the sisterhood I found with her. Sisterhood is a bonding feeling of connectivity and closeness. That's what I love about our friendship: there is deep understanding and constant support. We each make the other feel secure and safe, there is no judgment or reservation.

The friendship we created is truly a gift. It's very special to me. It is one of the best dishes that has been served during the *omakase* of my life. Because of it, the table we shared three times a day for those two long weeks was no longer cold. The warmth of friendship cast away the alienation that I felt on that first day.

Yes, each one of us has our own story to tell, our own journey to take. The journey is coloured by seasons of trials and triumphs; fear and courage; and trauma and healing. I specifically adore the word 'season' as it talks about a *period of time*, not an overnight event.

Going through a season takes patience and hope. We must be mindful of what our heart is saying to us. There will be fears and we will wonder how things will unfold, but that's the very opportunity we are given to rise above and take control, to fight to change the situation for the better. Throughout YCAB's journey, we have maintained hope and faith that our chefs will appear when we need them so that they can help us build the menu of the day. It is the chefs who have determined our 'seasonal menus'; they are the ones who will pave our road to legacy. Their offerings and knowledge have come together to lead YCAB down the path of integration and sustainability. Steering us from season to season, to stay hopeful for sunshine in the days of our dreadful winter of doubts.

We need to have courage and embrace each course of the *omakase*. Only after partaking in the entire meal – our whole life – will we be able to look back and make sense of the entire array of flavours. We will hopefully understand that the bitterness is needed to escalate the sweetness that follows it, and how a flavour is affected by the ones that follow and precede it.

The art is how we perceive our life's situation – how we pull it all together, making the best of it all. Above all, creating time amidst our struggles and triumphs to be with our loved ones is key. Family can be our relatives, or people that we bond with, such as friends. In YCAB's case, family includes colleagues, volunteers, interns, donors and partners.

Family and friends are the gifts of life. At both the personal and organisational level, I think this remains true. It is one of the meanings of being in the presencing state. Long before I had been introduced to the presencing concept at MIT, I had learned it from the very best source, my own beloved mother. It is the value that I most want to pass down to my children and their children.

What I have learned is this: stay calm during *fubuki*; stay mindful throughout the courses of life's *omakase*; and remain hopeful that the one true Chef will arrive in time to help you make sense of everything. Looking at life from the perspective of eternity while still living it is a good perspective to embrace.

That's why those questions mattered to me, those existential questions of meaning and purpose. We are created in the image of God, and because of this we have our values and a sense of eternity. Only when we look at our existence as a whole can we see the purpose of our being and understand the seasons of our lives.

'There's no excuse not to participate: you do good and make money. That's the beauty of social enterprise, the beauty of hope for the sustainable betterment of our world.'

JOURNEY TO IMPACT

'Mum, does YCAB work with any water organisations?' Phil asked me one afternoon.

'I can surely find out. Why, what do you have in mind?' I was curious.

Phil explained that he had to do a community project for school, and that his group wanted to provide piped water to a village with a few thousand households just outside Jakarta. The village is called Kampung Lemo and is located in the Tangerang area. I was surprised by their ambition and thought that it might be wise for them to embark on a smaller-scale project. I gently broached my concerns with Phil, 'That's a huge deal, even a formal NGO would need to work very hard to make it happen. Have you considered how much money you will need to raise, and the level of project management that will be required? Are you sure you want to do this? You might be in over your head.'

Phil calmly replied, 'Don't worry, Mum. We have a great team and we are sure that we can achieve this.' I could sense his confidence.

But surely, I thought to myself, *he really doesn't know what he's getting himself into.*

To have an impact on 5,000 households? I still couldn't wrap my head around the scale of their ambition. What was motivating them? Was it that the project would look good on their university applications or did they really want to make a difference through this mandatory community project? Whatever their motivation, the project offered a brilliant chance for them to learn. While it is true that water provision is not my area of expertise, I vowed to help the group by putting them in touch with people who would be able to help them.

'Phil, tell me something. What difference are you trying to make? In our lingo, what is your intended "impact"?' I was still trying to grasp why his group had chosen this particular project. 'Is it really necessary to try and reach that many homes? That's the real question.' I quickly thought more about the details and asked, 'Do you need to bring piped water directly into each home, or would it be enough to provide a communal piped water source for everyone?'

'Wow, Mum, you have so many questions,' he smiled. 'We haven't gotten that far yet. But, yes, we need a sizeable number of households to show the seriousness of this project.' Phil continued in a more serious tone, 'Ideally, we want to bring piped water directly into each home, but first we need to understand how difficult the construction will be and how long it will take to build. The thing is, Mum, we have limited time to spend on this project. We need to make sure that we are realistic about what we can achieve in the time that we have. Then we must focus on our university applications and our final IB exams.'

He really is a very sensible young man, I thought to myself. Then I outlined the obvious steps in planning social intervention for him. The first thing is always assessment. This covers the basics such as locating the area, understanding the needs of the people you want to impact and anticipating the challenges. After an assessment has been made, we usually move on to project calculation. The right project partner needs to be chosen (in Phil's case someone who can help with the construction), and then funds need to be raised to complete the project.

In YCAB's case, choosing the right partner is key. In some cases, we have been successful; however in a few instances, we could possibly have made better choices. There are many reasons that project partners might not see eye to eye. For example, a misalignment of mission or different expectations for project outcomes or an incorrect assessment of a partner's project management capability.

Project management is a relatively rigid process. It is a structured delivery checklist that matches a predetermined schedule. The truth is that what makes a successful project manager is the ability to see where in the schedule unpredictable delays might occur. Experience and maturity are very valuable assets that help a manager navigate any project well. While maturity is essential, so is the ability to balance the interests of all the parties involved in the project; a touch of cultural sensitivity is also invaluable. Things get even more complicated when corporate egos are involved. Sometimes corporations confuse the desire to make a difference with the pursuit of recognition and glory. Great project management can make it possible to achieve both aims. It's never easy, but it can be considered the real art of humanitarian work, I suppose.

We need to keep an open mind, even when we come across partners who treat programme implementers unfairly. There are those who ask us to deliver work that is not in the budget, but they are nothing compared to those who one day casually call to completely change the direction of the project. Sometimes their reasoning is understandable; maybe they want the project to better align with their board's direction and they have just realised there's a better way to do that. But sometimes the reasons are not that rational; they may have simply changed their minds about how the project might better attract good media exposure for their company. Many a time YCAB has been cornered into holding unbudgeted press conferences or kick-off events that had not been previously planned. I always hate when companies are trapped between social value and image creation. We all know it is not unusual for companies to spend one dollar in corporate social responsibility (CSR) yet use five dollars to promote it.

There are also partners who come up with radical ideas to commercialise the social activity after the project is already halfway completed. Some companies expect us to deliver more than what was initially agreed upon. In one extreme example, we have worked with a multinational in the past that expected YCAB to pay all the advance costs to the suppliers, and if we didn't comply they would withdraw their support from the project. YCAB is a non-profit organisation; we cannot afford such huge upfront costs. That's why we partner with big businesses in the first place. Such instances create unnecessary tension. Handling the delicate balance of promise and purpose, as well as ego and integrity, takes a wealth of maturity, understanding and patience.

Nothing can really surprise us at this point. We always do our best, but prepare for the worst. We have learned that it is best to plan for any contingency. The exposure we have had to issues we didn't expect has given us valuable experience, creating a kind of sophistication in our project management. We have learnt something new with each challenge we have faced. So maybe we should thank our more difficult partners. Because I am an optimist, I believe positives always come out of negatives. And yes, these challenges have sometimes held back our success but, like everything in life, having to work hard for our success has taught us so much more. Only through fire, people say, can gold truly shine.

Having come through the 'fire', we can celebrate the acquisition of real insights and an understanding of the complexities of partnerships. We have learnt that constant communication is crucial. In addition to this, we now also know that there should be a project sponsor who coordinates the project at YCAB headquarters to assist and be as accountable as the project implementer in the field. This might be basic knowledge for some people, but we didn't know this until we learnt it the hard way.

We really cherish the friendships we have fostered with the

majority of our partners through the years. Sponsors or partners that have been with us for years really have become our good friends, and together we become ecosystem enablers, enabling change and enabling other NGOs that cover things that we don't. These NGOs become our good friends, too.

In our experience, finding NGO partners can happen accidently. Sometimes the way the connection is made is almost unbelievable, but we are always very grateful when it happens. One such successful project partnership is seeding YCAB's international programme. The opportunity arose when I, as the Young Global Leader (YGL), was matched with the winner of British Council's Global Change Maker (GCM). The idea was for the YGL to mentor the GCM winner. It meant that I had the privilege of meeting a young and energetic social entrepreneur from Myanmar, Xin. She was only nineteen when I met her. We quickly made a deep connection based on passion for education provision for the poor. It was the beginning of YCAB working not only in Myanmar, but also in Afghanistan, Pakistan and Uganda. Later we also worked in Mongolia and Laos, but under a different model. After our strategy focus shifted to the least developed countries in Southeast Asia, we exited from programmes in countries outside of the Southeast Asian region after two years of operation.

Besides the strategic shift, we also found our local partners could not deliver as expected. Just like in dating, when things don't work out, we move on. But with Myanmar, we are ready for an engagement. This is a long-term commitment and we're happy to continue to work together. What's missing in Myanmar is the business component. We have not discovered a business that can sustain the education programme there. We have made a number of attempts, but so far none of them have been successful. More effort is needed, but we are confident that we'll get it right soon.

So partnership isn't only about chemistry. It's important, but it's not everything. Discipline and alignment of values and goals are also imperative: discipline in keeping the governance and programme checklist, and alignment in our mission and goals for impact.

This is what I needed to share with Phil. For his water project he would need to establish a partnership with a water organisation. The alignment of mission between Phil's group and the organisation partner is crucial. They must have a clear outline of deliverables of success. Even after they find this perfect partner, there's still one more thing they absolutely need. In order to achieve their mission, they need the money for the project.

※ ※ ※

'Does Joey have a suit, Mum?' Phil asked me.

'Yes, but I hope it still fits him. It's actually your suit from *Om* ('uncle' in Bahasa) Dede's wedding, remember? Why do you want to know?'

'The fundraising gala for the water project is next week and the dress code is formal,' Phil explained to me. 'I don't want Joey to feel as though he doesn't fit in.'

I smiled and nodded, 'Don't worry, Phil. We'll get him suited and booted.' Deep inside, I giggled at their seriousness about holding this fundraising gala night, which was being held in a four-star hotel near their school.

I couldn't help but think back to YCAB's first fundraising night. It wasn't until 2009, ten years after our establishment, that we held our first fundraising event. We called it the Angel of Change Night, which is now held annually. The name represents the opportunity that everyone has, to be an angel to create change with YCAB. Before that, it had never occurred to me that inviting friends to an event and asking them to pay for a plate or a table was the route we wanted to take in raising our funds. All I knew was to develop businesses so they could help cover the cost of YCAB's mission.

Eighteen years ago when I started YCAB, it all seemed plain and simple. The plan was to make money through the companies (YCAB's business units) and let the foundation perform the social activities with the support of the companies. The idea was to absorb some of the back-office costs of the foundation. From our auditor, EY, we later learned that this particular set-up between a foundation and its subsidiary companies has a term. It is called 'share resources' or 'share services', which means that some services such as accounting, legal, human resources and IT are underwritten by the companies, and the resources (the people) of these respective departments are considered to be volunteering their time to provide services to the foundation.

I thought it was a very good arrangement that all non-profits should follow. But there was no specific term for the kind of ventures we were in back then; it was just running both a foundation and its supporting companies. Only in the last decade have people started to put us under this new category called 'social enterprise'. It actually sounds right, I like the term. It is as if the term were made for YCAB.

To laypeople it seems that YCAB is visionary and ahead of its time. The truth is, I didn't really plan for YCAB to become a social enterprise. How could I have planned something that didn't even have a name at that time? I purely followed my gut feeling, my entrepreneurial spirit. I always thought that if anyone should fund my calling, it should be me. I had to find some way to finance my mission. And making money through business was the only thing I could think of. If we made the money, no one else could tell us how to spend it. The idea is simple: YCAB needs to be independent.

After years of following this model, YCAB is now considered to be one of Indonesia's classic examples of social enterprise. We love this. We readily embrace that notion. Even though it wasn't intentional, the concept of social entrepreneurship had been apparent at YCAB's core since the beginning.

※ ※ ※

'Vera, you've been working on your mission for years now,' said one of my good friends, Lisa Schad. 'We've been watching you and I think it's time you let us show our support.'

'What do you mean?' I responded, curious as to what she was actually offering.

'You need to share with us, give us the opportunity to support YCAB,' she explained.

That's the nicest thing anyone could ever say to me. It made me think of what Abraham Maslow said about people being basically altruistic. In his terms, when people are 'fully actualised', they need to help and give. People need to leave behind a trail of deeds. The offer from Lisa and my realisation changed everything I had ever thought about funding my mission, and it sounded so dignified.

The funny thing is, my friends think I've been selfish. They joke about how I must want heaven all to myself. Although I believe that people end up in heaven due to God's grace and not because of their deeds, I was flattered by their kindness. My friends want to be involved. They want the opportunity to give. Realising this really changed my perspective. They're truly my angels.

From my friends' requests I learned that there are people out there who want to give. However, many of them aren't sure to whom they should give. There's always a trust issue. People want to make sure their money ends up in the right hands, doing the right thing as promised.

To some extent, I think my conversation with Lisa really helped me conquer my fear. I had been afraid to ask my friends for help, especially in the form of money for YCAB. I never wanted my friends to feel obligated. I didn't want them to think that every time I reached out to them it was only because I wanted a donation. The way in which Lisa framed it made me realise that people wanted to stand behind YCAB. The Angel of Change Night was born then.

Maybe it was my unconscious fear that steered YCAB into

becoming a social enterprise. The truth is there was no genius plan to become a great social enterprise, after all. I wanted to run the foundation my way and I was afraid to ask for money; it was easier to find a way to make the money myself. Yes, I have an entrepreneurial spirit within me that keeps driving YCAB to be independent. But, what's the underlying aspect of this spirit? Is it only my fear? Then I think to myself, so what if it is fear that's driving me? It has proven to be a very good motivator. I don't think I should be ashamed of admitting this. This fear is a positive fear: it has helped me overcome all the challenges by finding innovative solutions.

We all have fears and we all have anxieties. Sometimes they are unavoidable and beyond our control. But the key is not to let them consume us. We should try and turn our fears into the power for good. Fear helped turn YCAB into a social enterprise eighteen years ago, it gave us the means to survive. So I learned that not all fears are bad; some fears are good.

Speaking of fear, I was worried for Phil and his fundraiser. Phil and his team were responsible for hosting the fundraising night, but I was the one with butterflies in my stomach. I was excited to see how they would make it work, gathering parents to buy tables and raising the money for the project. In addition to that, they had managed to collect some art works to be auctioned.

Selling seats or plates is one thing, but pulling off an auction is another. Especially an auction meant to appeal to a bunch of donors who have already paid to attend the function. Some of them must have been thinking, *I already paid to be here and now they have put me in a situation where I need to give more* or, in Bahasa, *ditodong.*

YCAB has never attempted to hold an auction. Maybe because I have always worried about how successful it would be, we never tried. For me, the time that goes into preparing for an auction seems like too much effort for an uncertain outcome.

Once I was invited to an amazingly successful auction night to benefit Alicia Keys' foundation. She's a big celebrity and her fundraising gala is always one of the highlights of the society calendar. I was honoured to be invited to her event in New York and had my $5,000 plate paid for by a friend of mine who is a big fan of Keys' work. I was quite intimidated as I walked the red carpet for the event. It looked like Oscars night: people were really dressed up, and there were celebrities in attendance. I had never seen so many cameras in one place in my life.

The line-up that night was breathtaking. Famous singers performed songs to entertain guests throughout the night. JAY-Z, Norah Jones and will.i.am were among them. Familiar faces, Hollywood actors and actresses donating their time. People were willing to pay tens thousands of dollars for a dinner with Matthew McConaughey, or lunch with Angelina Jolie, or a private golf lesson with Tiger Woods. I think those were the coolest auction items I had ever seen. There were no paintings or rare wines, it was all people for people.

It was a breathtaking night, and it was really inspiring. But then I thought to myself, *I'm not sure I could host a night on a scale like this. I shouldn't even attempt it.* I guess that's the problem. For me the bar has been raised too high. I have seen how a great fundraiser is hosted and until I can match or better it, I don't want to try. But the question is, when will I be able to arrange such an amazing event? I don't know. Maybe never, as I am still not convinced that it is the route YCAB is destined to take. I don't think I have the right skill set to put together an awesome auction like that.

But Alicia Keys did it. She did it so well that it discouraged me from trying to emulate her. And I know there are many other non-profits out who hold successful nights like Alicia Keys' fundraiser but on a smaller scale, but I don't think it's YCAB's thing. I would rather invest to expand our businesses and make money that way than spend an entire year planning a fundraising auction.

Planning fundraising is indeed time consuming and difficult as it has to be innovative, too. In my head, there's this two by two matrix for a fundraising formula with the two axes being proceeds (funds raised) and profile. In the case of Alicia Keys, her fundraising galas prove to be both high-profile and high-proceeds, raising millions of dollars for charity. Ultimately, we want Alicia Keys' formula: high-profile, high-proceeds. But in our experience, not all fundraising turns out that way.

High-proceeds is the obvious target, but will it be high- or low-profile? I wouldn't really mind a low-profile event if it was also high-proceeds!

Some of our annual events are actually the opposite. They are high-profile, but low-proceeds. This is acceptable if, and only if, everything is entirely done by the event owner and we just act as the beneficiary of the proceeds. I don't mind that at all. As long as we don't need to put down capital or find sponsors for the event, I think that's quite decent. Events such as these, in our experience, usually come with really good media exposure. But would I be willing to plan for a high-profile, low-proceeds event myself? Probably not. It's too much trouble and it's not worth the time. It's needless to say that no one should ever consider a low-profile, low-proceeds event!

However, I have been surprised in the past. An event that I thought would be low-profile, high-proceeds turned to be high-profile, high-proceeds. YCAB has been involved in some unusual fundraising activities, such as the one brought to us by our dear friend, Scott Thompson.

Scott popped in to YCAB's office one day and explained his idea to run from Bali to Jakarta in twenty days. That's a distance of 1,250 kilometres, meaning he would need to run at least 60 kilometres per day. It's equivalent to doing thirty marathons back to back. I thought to myself, 'Can someone really do this?'

There were obvious doubts that any human could pull off something like this. But it didn't take long for Scott to convince us. With so much excitement following his day-to-day running, we knew somehow Scott would make it. And he did. Not only did he prove me wrong for doubting his ability, but he proved that an event like this could have a huge media impact.

It was a very nice surprise when the media responded to Scott's effort to run for Indonesian school dropouts. His journey started with a pretty humble kickoff, but ended in huge media fanfare. When two years after his Bali to Jakarta run, Scott decided to undertake another crazy challenge, we knew he would garner more media attention. This time he wanted to cycle a *becak* (traditional Indonesian trishaw) 2,650 kilometres from Aceh to Jakarta in twenty-one days.

I had my concerns about this challenge as well. After his successful Bali to Jakarta run, I was no longer worried about Scott having the physical strength to complete the task; he had more than proved his capability and determination. I was more concerned about the massive forest fire that was raging across three provinces in Sumatra that he would go through. The amount of ash and smoke could really kill him. But again, he was *bandel* (Bahasa for 'stubborn'). He completed the journey and ended up earning a place in the *Guinness Book of World Records*.

Success is one thing, but Scott literally made history with his record-breaking achievement. Scott's challenge stands as a testament to fundraising through extreme sport. It was an extreme display of human strength and true sportsmanship in order to do good and raise more than a million dollars. Because of Scott, sweat-based fundraising is what people think YCAB does best. It has helped create a high-profile, high-proceeds success formula for YCAB. We raised IDR6.7 billion (approximately USD520,000), Scott broke the Guinness World Record and subsequently received the prestigious Order of the British Empire (OBE) title.

However, there's another way that YCAB is involved in sweat-based fundraising. Growing our businesses to support our mission is pretty 'sweaty' work too. Nothing extreme like Scott's achievements, but fundraising internally, from the companies under YCAB, is something we work very hard on and we will continue to do so in order to be sustainable.

In 2008, our businesses at that point had actually underwritten

100 per cent of back-office costs. But as the foundation kept expanding, there were ups and downs in the coverage of those shared back-office costs. The only way to create stability is for the businesses to grow even faster to catch up with the foundation's programme expansion. Until we achieve this, we will continue to struggle. That being said, our focus is now two-pronged. First is to create the stability through change management and restructuring of the whole YCAB group; and the second is to aggressively grow the businesses while at the same time raising social investment funds to additionally support programme costs. That's my biggest challenge. And I'd like to do it slowly but surely.

The idea is to create a sustainable channel on three levels. Level one is to create long-term funding to cover our core costs – the core costs being the minimum cost to maintain YCAB's core team and core programme. At level two, we hope to continue to grow all our businesses to cover 100 per cent of non-core or other programme costs. And of course, at level three we will continue developing partnerships with multinationals and corporations through both the sponsorship of special projects and the philanthropic investment programmes.

Through the years, we have seen an amazing escalation in the number of our partners. We always love working with them, but it's just not sustainable funding. Corporations have their own mandate, and at some point, if and when their direction changes, the programme we have started with them may suffer. This makes social investment the best route for independence and sustainability.

What can be better than knowing your money is being used to alleviate poverty while you enjoy a financial return? That's double joy, knowing that your money can change people's lives for the better while you receive interest upon your principal investment at the same time.

Now everyone can be an Angel of Change. As a giver or investor, everyone can create change for the better. Social investment is an inclusive platform that allows 'shy givers' to lend their money to YCAB so that we can use it to do good. There's no excuse not to participate: you do good and make money. That's the beauty of social enterprise, the beauty of hope for the sustainable betterment of our world.

But the night of Phil's auction was different. It was a special night. I had a feeling that his group's auction would be a success. I was already so proud as a parent knowing that Phil and his team had managed so much, and I am sure the other parents were, too. I had promised myself that I would buy something at the auction to support Phil. I would have bid even if there was nothing I wanted. I am sure that every parent at the event had made the same promise.

Step one complete. Phil and his friends had raised the funds. The real battle was still ahead: implementation and proof of impact.

※ ※ ※

'How much did you raise, Son?' I asked with a curious smile.

'That's the problem, Mum,' Phil replied with a sigh. I could detect trouble. 'We wanted to raise enough for the entire *kampung*, but we have to settle for just some of the households,' he paused a little before continuing in a more upbeat tone, 'I guess we just need to improvise!'

'What do you have in mind?' I was curious.

'I think we will have to settle with the provision of communal wells instead of piped water to each household. It's cheaper to build and costs less to maintain.'

Upon hearing that Phil's team had to adapt to the reality of financial constraints, my mind raced back to the year 2005. It was the first fashion show for charity ever held in Indonesia. Sebastian – Indonesia's top haute couture designer who is also my good friend who made my wedding gown – came up with the idea to use his annual show to raise funds. Truthfully, I expected more from this gala. But we had to settle with the reality, too. We learned that although the *crème de la crème* of Indonesia's society loved to be seen in the front row, their charitable spirit still needed to be encouraged. I think it was simply a new concept to them. Those VVIPs were used to being given free access. The idea of 'buying' their front-row seats was completely alien to them. I remember Sebastian and I faced a challenging time explaining the concept, not only to the VVIPs but to the media as well. We ended up selling more front-rows to corporations than fashionistas.

Tragic, but it was the cost of educating society about giving. In the years that followed, I think we managed to raise the bar and shape fashion society so that they are more giving. Someone had to start something a bit outside of the box in order to encourage change and Sebastian took that risk. Since then, YCAB has enjoyed the amazing annual opportunity to fundraise with Sebastian. He really has set the tone for other Indonesian designers, both in terms of design and inspiring them to integrate philanthropy into their work.

'Mum, I think you were right.' Phil snapped me out of my wandering thoughts.

'Right about what, Sweetie?'

'You were right when you said that we were too ambitious,' he grinned a little and continued, 'With the money we've got, we can only reach 500 families now.'

'That's totally fine, Son! It's already great that your project can reach out to 500 households. Imagine if each household has four or five people, then you're talking about impact for 2,000 to 2,500 people,' I said in an encouraging tone before dropping the bomb, 'What's more important though is for you to discuss with your teammates the project's KPIs, the key performance indicators, and what success looks to you. Eventually, you will need to figure out how to measure the real impact.'

'Mum, the impact is quite obvious. It brings something out of nothing. And that something is access to clean water. And because of it, their life improves,' reasoned Phil.

Improvement of life. Phil said it well. If I were to slip in a word into his sentence, it would be the term 'quality'. The improvement of their *quality* of life.

I believe in quality. It is the depth of a programme that creates the change in human life. We know this now, but we had to learn it the hard way.

YCAB's first programme, HeLP (Healthy Lifestyle Promotion), is pretty unique because it is difficult to measure the effect of soft-skills training in preventing youth from engaging in risky behaviour, such as drug abuse. When we are dealing with only 3-5 per cent of youth with the likelihood of experimenting with drugs, it is unrealistic to claim that if they don't end up experimenting with drugs, it is solely because of our programme.

There are too many variables, and one cannot make a conclusive assessment without implementing serious long-term research using a gold standard such as a randomised control trial. In my opinion, other research approaches are also possible but they aren't as convincing as those that use a control group.

In the case of primary prevention, experts conclude that it is almost impossible to make such a claim. So it did take us some time to figure out how to measure the intended impact of our HeLP programme. Then we decided to do pre- and post-tests to measure changes in participants' level of knowledge, attitude and behaviour.

Over time, we learned that output, outcome and impact are three different things. Compared to HeLP, measuring the two other programmes, HoLD and HOpE (covering education and economic empowerment respectively), is more straightforward.

YCAB measures impact as follows: output is the number of people exposed to the programme; outcome is the result of the programme; and impact is the change it brings and what that change means to the community or the society at large. Change here has to be systematic and sustainable, that's the only way it can be meaningful.

Here's an example from our education pillar: the number of young people enrolled in the programme is output; the number of graduates is the outcome. So if 100 people enrolled in Rumah Belajar, the learning centre, and all 100 students stay in the programme, that's output. From those who stay and sit the exam, only 90 pass, then that's the outcome. The impact is determined by the number of graduates who go on to get jobs and become financially independent or *mandiri*. The obvious change is this: we want people to go from a school dropout to an independent person with a future.

As for the economic empowerment (HOpE), the measurement of impact is even clearer. From the extensive conversations we have had with programme beneficiaries and our programme investors, we are pretty set on what to measure. We all think that tracking changes in the recipients' daily income is a good indicator of improvement.

We found that our beneficiaries' income doubled within twelve to fifteen months of receiving access to a small amount of capital for their businesses. The average daily income of USD1.80 per person per day went up to between USD2.80–3.30 per person per day. This means we have raised them out of the World Bank's standard of poverty, which is USD2 per person per day. But the question remains: is it enough? To what level of income do we need to bring them? Of course, we want to assist them until they reach a middle-class income. But what really constitutes a middle-class income in Indonesia? This simple question has an incredibly complex answer. But that's another case for another time. However, we suspect it is somewhere between USD5–6 per person per day.

The point is this: we have done our best to understand impact. It is not perfect, but we have tried our best to measure it. We are very open to learning more, as I personally believe learning never ends as long as we live. At the end of the day, if I had to choose between quantity and quality, I will always choose quality. Quality is found in the human story – how our programme improves and transforms the beneficiaries' lives.

I know quality gives us the depth of intervention and impact, but in my weak moments I sometimes feel divided. My ambition demands quantity. That makes me want both quality *and* quantity.

So the next important question is, what strategy can achieve this? We talked about this with the team and we decided that we want to deepen our intervention in the areas where our business units are already established and concentrate there. We also want to open new territory to reach more people, but we should only do that when we have a sponsor to do it with.

The challenge is to strike a balance between quality and quantity, and to choose what to prioritise, as this affects the focus of the team. Since the word 'priority' implies that one aspect is inherently more important than another, I believe quality should be our choice. There is, however, a constant battle in my heart. I must keep telling myself to accept that we can only chase quantity – which means expansion – when we have sponsors for it.

But one thing always haunts us. Are we prepared to close down a Rumah Belajar, for example, when the sponsorship expires and our business has yet to grow in that area to cover its cost? It just breaks my heart to have to close down a programme. Our position is never to close, and we have found ourselves setting up businesses to cover the ongoing costs. In one strategic meeting, our board members ended up adopting the programmes we were supposed to vote to close. Is this healthy? I don't think so. But the battle continues.

Every time my quantity ambition takes control of my mind, my heart tends to stick firmly with quality. I always remind myself that quantity is just statistics. But quality speaks about the real change we see in people's lives. When a scavenger becomes an entrepreneur, or a domestic helper who dropped out of school becomes the best technician at a Samsung service centre in all of Southeast Asia. That's the story of real life. That's the reason we do what we do.

Quantity has no story to tell. But Phil's 500 households having access to clean water is both quantity and quality. Why can't all social programmes be this straightforward and achieve on both levels? Are we in the wrong business? The provision of education for the poor is one thing, but tracking whether they become *mandiri* is another. However, tracking how educated children contribute to the welfare of their families is more complicated and can only be measured in the long term. How can we simplify this?

※ ※ ※

'I was selling vegetables at the market and one day I was robbed,' Ibu Nani began her story. 'They stole my truck, which was worth more than IDR1 million. I guess it was fate.' Her eyes dimmed. 'We didn't know what to do; we had no more money to put into our business. Then a few days later, a neighbour came and asked me whether I would join her group to get a small loan offered by YCAB Cooperative. I took that opportunity to rebuild my business,' her eyes sparkled as she finished her story.

Ibu Nani is one of the 150,000 women micro-entrepreneurs who have been given access to a small loan to grow their business by YCAB Cooperative. However, not everyone grows their business like Ibu Nani. When she rebuilt, she went from being a vegetable vendor in the market to supplying vegetables to the market. She used to sell a motorcycle-load of vegetables, and now she operates her own mini truck and hires her husband to drive and supply vegetables to the whole market. They became business partners. It's a great story to tell. However, the story doesn't end there.

The best part of Ibu Nani's story is this: one of her twelve children, the eldest daughter from the surviving six siblings, went to college. Although she didn't finish college because she got married and had a baby, she managed to rise in social status, so to speak. She now runs an online store that rents out traditional Indonesian outfits. With the money she makes, she has purchased education insurance for her two children to ensure they will have university-level education. Isn't that amazing? For me personally, I think that's the value of YCAB being transferred to the beneficiary of the programme. This, I believe, is the real impact of the programme that makes all loans conditional on the recipients' children furthering their education.

Conversely, I believe real impact goes far beyond how a programme touches one life. It can transform one person's mind and heart so that they systemically create change in their families. Muntaka, for instance, was a scavenger who went on to study at college. He graduated at the top of his mechanic class and enrolled in an advanced course with Honda. There again, he finished the course with flying colours, and his results landed him a job as a car mechanic. After working for several years, his ambition grew. He continued to work while studying at college and he aspires to own his own mechanical service centre one day. I truly believe he can achieve this. When he really makes it, his children won't be the children of a scavenger but the children of an entrepreneur! That's change. Imagine the confidence his children will have one day, knowing that their father is a self-made man and because of that, they will have access to an education.

Public policymakers, however, probably don't see things as we see them. They like what we offer, but they want to see numbers. They need good statistics to stay in power. Whatever is achieved is fine, as long as it makes them look good. It's a different story with programme funders and investors. Investors are happy as soon as they get their investment back plus interest. This is a normal desire for a normal market, but not for impact investors, I think. As the 'market' is not for profit, it should be impact first, not profit first. There are many investors who can't, or won't, understand this. They want both impact and commercial market rate returns on their investment. Not many social enterprises can deliver both, hence the mismatch between expectation and reality.

Grant makers are another story again. They operate under a certain mandate, and they are usually happy when all KPIs are met on schedule and to budget. The funny thing is that they all expect the programme to be sustainable after a period of time, believing that the local people will underwrite it or run it sustainably for them. The reality is nothing will continue to work when funding stops (unless it's adopted by the local people or the government). Local people, in most cases, won't automatically assume responsibility and continue the good work that has started there.

Funders or grant makers tend to forget there should be an economic empowerment of some sort, either to an NGO or the local community to inherit the programme. Basically, there should be an income-generating activity that covers the costs of the programme. That's simple maths. Without it, no programme will continue to run. That's what social entrepreneurship is all about. That is the reason why I believe social entrepreneurship brings hope for sustainable change. Not because social entrepreneurship itself is a hope, but through it we can see everything else, everything that will ensure sustainability and growth.

Let me give you one example. In 2011, Chevron became our first social investor, investing in education and small capital for a community near their geothermal site in Gunung Salak, a two-hour drive from Jakarta. They invested USD150,000 and we used USD50,000 of it to set up two classes of Rumah Belajar, a sewing class and a computer class. The rest was to be disbursed to the more than 1,000 women micro-entrepreneurs in the area. Once we hit the breakeven point, both Rumah Belajar and the microfinance operations were subsequently covered by the income generated. And not only that, in the third year we had USD50,000 extra in savings and the community decided to use it to add more Rumah Belajar classes. They chose to establish another sewing class and an English-language class.

The programme there was not only sustainable, it was remarkable; remarkable in terms of how it keeps giving birth to new programmes periodically while preserving the initial capital, the amount invested. That's the power of income-generating activity, the power of profit.

Profitability is sustainability. No matter how many social activists or social entrepreneurs seem allergic to use the word 'profit', it is profit that can give us the independence to do what we want to do. There's freedom to use the money that we make for social good, and only social good. I understand why some can't help but be against those who use the money generated from social investment for their own benefit. Profit from social investment has to serve the mission, not the shareholders or the initial investors/funders alone.

I know my ideas may not sound mainstream to some, but I stand my ground. My perspective is determined by my position as a social entrepreneur. Being a dedicated social entrepreneur is different from being a big corporation that wants to bring positive impact through their businesses. There's nothing wrong with corporations taking this approach; in fact it is to be commended. But it's also important to remember that their first responsibility is still to their shareholders, not their beneficiaries. While my perspective comes from an impact-first position, corporations are still motivated by a profit-first position. The difference is that the first and foremost motivation of social entrepreneurship is to do social good. There should first be impact, then financial gain. It is therefore creating social change by using business tools and business thinking. That's where the entrepreneurial angle comes in and that's the social entrepreneurship that I know.

Yes, one has to cover costs and make money, but all profit (or at least the majority of it) that a social enterprise makes must go back to serve its mission. Call me a traditionalist, but I think that's the right way. I take inspiration from Matthew 6:21, 'For where your treasure is, there your heart will be'. So for those who claim to be a social entrepreneur, their hearts must first be anchored to the mission. And that's the only way one can stay faithful to one's passion and calling to serve in the first place. Yes, there's a lot of 'fortune at the bottom of the pyramid' as Prahalad argued in his book, but social entrepreneurs need a control system to check where their hearts really lie – on the fortune or on the service to humanity. In many cases, the defining line is so thin that they may stray from their mission, their first love.

So then, is water provision a good social business? Will Phil and his team see it that way? I hope so. This is something the next generation needs to see: they can innovate solutions to lift others out of poverty while sustaining their living through the profit earned. Phil's water project only serves 500 households. Don't misunderstand me, that's a great number for highschoolers to achieve, but the reality is there are hundreds of millions of households worldwide that are without access to clean, let alone piped, water. But helping 500 households is always better than nothing.

Impact has to be tracked to be meaningful. Social entrepreneurship makes impact possible as it makes all the money needed to serve a mission. It gives the freedom to grow when profit permits, and at the same time gives the resources to deepen the understanding of what really makes a difference to the beneficiaries. At the end of the day, a social entrepreneur can only do so much, and cannot help everybody. We can only help those who want to fight for change; without that fight nothing sustainable can be achieved. Together, we can create a deeper impact that lasts through generations.

That's what YCAB intends to do. From our years of implementing programmes, we realise we can only shift from good to great by enabling like-minded non-profit or social enterprises. It's our mission to help non-profits transition into social enterprise; this way the work that we do can be sustainable. I feel the time is right to crack the poverty problem, and the more social enterprises there are, the better the state of the world will become.

We all know that there is only so much we can do alone, but together we can do greater things. Coming to the end of YCAB's second decade, I think the more refined mission for myself is to create a more conducive ecosystem for social enterprises to grow and provide platforms for policy, knowledge, partnership and funding.

The lack of funding and resources is the issue that every organisation faces. It's a classic challenge but without a facilitative policy, we can't go very far. After policy comes the funding issue. With social investment, it is possible to grow without waiting for government subsidies or grants, as we can tap into the market of investors and givers.

In my opinion, there are at least four kinds of givers. Those who give freely: the philanthropic giver trusts that the organisation to which they have given their money will make the most of it. However, even if they give philanthropically, there's a growing number of givers who want their giving to be 'preserved' sustainably. That's why they call themselves 'capital preservation givers'. It's the first category with a twist.

The second kind of giver is still philanthropic but they expect to see change, they follow through and want to see how their contribution is used. The third and fourth category, they're more hybrid: they lend their money. The third kind of giver will require only their principal money back, and they are happy as long as they know their money is used for a sustainable programme. The fourth kind of giver will want their money back, plus interest. I call the people in the fourth category 'shy givers'. In the end, they all create change, it's just their expectations that are different.

With social entrepreneurship, I believe funding has never been easier, as long as our programmes offer business feasibility and clear impact. After funding, comes the harder part: impact measurement. This is difficult, but it is the most meaningful part of what we do, it's the motivation. Impact needs to be seen clearly from both the doers or enablers like us, and the beneficiaries' side.

Partnerships are like marriages. There should be an alignment of values, strong commitment and a sense of responsibility in bringing about change, in addition to the passion for the mission. The passion may fade away when difficulties arise at the implementation level, but a strong will can carry it through. Both sides must understand that the ultimate focus is to serve the beneficiaries with the ultimate aim of creating change in their lives.

Selecting the right partner is therefore the beginning of success. Since we all want sustainable success, having the right business model guarding the mission is the pivotal answer to sustainability. Fundraising becomes part of the life of a social enterprise – either raising the funds internally (from business units) or externally, through partnerships or crowdfunding, we must observe the four quadrants of the proceeds and profile matrix, where effort and results can be predicted and justified.

Money is one important element in creating change, but it is not everything. Aiming for high-profile, high-proceeds is ideal, but one must settle for anything in between the four quadrants (except-low profile, low-proceeds). Money does matter, but relationships between programme partners matter more in the long term. Without the right people possessing the right capabilities and the right motivations to implement on the ground, even the best mission will not breed meaningful impact.

Lastly, the measurement of impact is everything to most donors and social investors. Without it, everything we do seems futile. I believe there is an equal value in both quantitative and qualitative measurement. I personally choose to combine the two when possible, as one approach can strengthen the other. Many will argue that it is not necessary, but others will agree that featuring the human story is powerful. The stories of Muntaka and Ibu Nani help paint a picture of lives transformed. In these stories, the real impact is laid bare.

Although they didn't manage to reach their initial goal, Phil's water project inspires me. He probably doesn't realise how much. I was quite envious, actually. His group had the right partner to work with, they successfully raised money for the project and lastly, the measurement of the impact was crystal clear. I wish all social programmes were as simple as this. I salute them for choosing the right project and I salute them for their resilience in continuing to strive despite the challenges they faced. I salute them for caring at such a young age.

'Just as YCAB is a gift to me, it becomes a gift to the people who benefit from its existence.'

chapter 8

EPILOGUE

The simple truth is that in order to be grateful we must first acknowledge that we have been given a gift.

Ravi Zacharias

I was contemplating whether or not to write this closing chapter. Some of the early readers of this book strongly urged me to do so. They told me that since this book tells a story of my eighteen-year journey in founding and growing YCAB, readers would naturally expect this book to close with a future outlook. Where will I be in another eighteen years? Where will I take YCAB? Will I still be driven to keep doing what I am doing now, or will there be a higher purpose beyond YCAB? Is there anything more to my existence?

I'm not sure whether or not it's a coincidence, but today is Thanksgiving. It is a day to give thanks to God for all His blessings in our life; for friends and family and all the work we manage to do in the fulfilment of our lives. I came across a beautiful short article by Ravi Zacharias with the title *A Prelude to Joy: A Thanksgiving Meditation*. He wrote about the real meaning of Thanksgiving and the reason for joy. He began with a story of a little girl who was excited to receive many gifts on her birthday. Since she was too young to read the notes attached to each gift, she asked an adult to tell her who had given her each gift, and she went to thank each one of them. The interesting thing was, she thanked them *before* opening the gifts. That's a sign of huge gratitude, and faith that she will like every gift given to her.

This little story makes me re-examine my own attitude and the orientation of my heart and mind towards Thanksgiving. In our lives, we tend to pick and choose the things for which we give thanks. Some of us fail to acknowledge that the main point is that we have been given a gift – what it is does not matter. Yet, sometimes we have the audacity to complain about some gifts because they are not according to our needs or taste.

I have seen people return gifts to the giver or ask for the gift to be exchanged for something else. It is outrageous, I know, but some people think this is acceptable behaviour. I have found myself exposed to such situations too many times already.

If you have never experienced this in your life, then you should consider yourself blessed. Come to think of it, I am to some extent blessed too, as witnessing such interactions has brought me to a different level of understanding about human behaviour; such people are in existence to contrast with other grateful people. Just like pain and pleasure, we can't understand the full extent of gratitude without experiencing ingratitude.

Of course, as givers we always want to give something useful to the recipient, but when they reject our gifts, it just hurts. The numbing pain I have experienced as the giver of rejected gifts is real.

There's a quote that goes like this: 'Gratefulness is riches; complaint is poverty'. Complaining prevents us from 'seeing the giver behind our gifts'. And this attitude naturally brings unhappiness to both the recipient and the giver. That's sad simply because if gifts bring unhappiness to both parties, then it defeats the very purpose of giving.

I'm having a moment of awakening here as I write this. I understand that our giving of thanks should not be driven by the kind of things we receive, but by the kindness and the thoughtfulness of the giver. The little girl's childish gratitude appreciates the giver more than the gift itself.

My dad used to say that we must sincerely appreciate what people give us or bring home for us from their travels, no matter how silly they sometimes are, because it is a sign of thoughtfulness and that they remembered us. That's what matters. And that's how I was brought up. So imagine the grim pain I feel when my gifts are returned or exchanged.

All this time I thought it was my fault because I hadn't given something expensive or branded enough. But now I realise that it was because the receiver had succumbed to their own bitterness. Their hearts are full of complaints and ungratefulness to the point of losing the ability to see the giver beyond the gift itself.

Then I question myself, what is the orientation of my heart? Is it more towards gratitude or complaint? This reminds me of a question my niece, Jackie, asked me a long time ago, 'How would you feel if YCAB were taken away from you?'

Her question really took me by surprise. I didn't know where she was coming from. It came totally out of the blue. But I really appreciated it; it was a hard question that forced me to review my perspective and examine my heart. For some reason, her question recalled a visual memory of a profound advertising page I had seen many times before. It is an advertisement for a famous watch brand, Patek Philippe. The ad always shows a picture of either a father and son, or a mother and daughter, with text underneath that reads 'You never really own a Patek Philippe, you're merely taking care of it for the next generation'. Isn't that a beautiful sentiment?

Not only beautiful; I also find it to be very true. I believe that nothing I have in this life is something that I actually own. I don't actually deserve anything that I have. Everything is a gift from God. And my job is to take care of these gifts and pass them down to the next generation.

So, with confidence I responded to Jackie, 'To my surprise, Jack, I think I would be fine. And you know why?' I paused a little and smiled at her rolling eyes, 'YCAB is a gift to my life. It is God's way of showing me the meaning and purpose of my life. If it were taken away, then I am sure there would be something else I could do, maybe even something greater than YCAB.' I quickly added, 'But even if there was nothing else, nothing of significance, I would go on living until my time is up. I would be grateful that I had been given the privilege to find joy and meaning through YCAB for whatever time I am allowed.'

Call it optimism or whatever, but I like to be positive. As a leader, I expect YCAB to grow from good to great and continue to be greater. By that, I mean I want YCAB to pass the sustainability phase and continue to march into the legacy creation phase – not just for me, but for Indonesia. The obvious motivation is to see YCAB grow in its love and its impact on the world, to always inspire the young generation – the millennials as they call them these days – to care for others and make a difference in this world.

For those who know me, my ambition is clear: YCAB must outlive me.

I know I will strive to do my best to make it happen in my lifetime, yet at the same time I need to be very mindful of my limitations. Guided by my two guiding principles, *ora et labora* and *omakase*, I know I am not alone. *Ora et labora* says that as long as I do my best, I know God will do the rest. And the *omakase* of life means that I know I will be satisfied with whatever is presented before me, simply because I trust the Chef. I have the confidence that the next dish of my life will be as impressive and as tasty as the one before.

Just as YCAB is a gift to me, it becomes a gift to the people who benefit from its existence. The first eighteen years have passed, and I am looking forward to the next eighteen years and beyond. All I know is that YCAB's future will come in a sparkling gift box with a bow of hope on top. Like that little girl, I don't need to know the contents of my gift box because I have faith in my Giver. So whatever is given to YCAB or to me, it doesn't matter. For I know and trust that my Giver knows what's best for each one of us.

ABOUT YCAB

YCAB is a social enterprise that aims to improve welfare through education and innovative financing. It runs several programmes that have reached 3.3 million underprivileged youth.

YCAB has several programmes, but of particular interest is HOpE, a microfinance scheme that lends money to female micro-entrepreneurs on the condition that their children remain in school. HOpE has granted more than 350,000 loans to date, resulting in thousands of school dropouts going back to school to complete their education. Some have attended government schools while others have enrolled in YCAB's Rumah Belajar (learning centres), which are spread across Indonesia.

YCAB is now exploring ways to implement the last link in its change model, to create a sustainable system wherein students who graduate and obtain employment – thanks to the education provided to them by YCAB – can pay it forward. It might be by giving back through direct donations or investing in a mutual fund to help grow and scale YCAB's mission-driven microfinance enabling YCAB to empower even more youths to take control of their future.

By 2020, YCAB aims to reach 5 million youths in six countries throughout Southeast Asia and raise USD50 million in social investment funds.

To learn more about YCAB and its achievements and goals, please visit www.ycabfoundation.org.

ABOUT VERONICA COLONDAM

Veronica Colondam is the founder and chief executive officer of YCAB Foundation. She holds double degrees in communication and public relations and an MSc. in social sciences from Imperial College London. She has also completed several leadership programmes including those offered by Harvard Kennedy School, Yale and MIT.

She has received many awards and abundant recognition for the work she has done with YCAB. She is the youngest-ever recipient of the UN-Vienna Civil Society Award, which she received in 2001. She became a World Economic Forum Young Global Leader in 2006. She was made a fellow of the Asia Society's 21 Young Leaders in 2007 and a Global Social Innovator Park Fellow in 2008.

She was named among Globe Asia's Most Powerful Women in Indonesia in 2007. Channel NewsAsia declared her Asia's Change Maker in 2009 and the Asian of the Year in 2010 and Forbes named her one of the 10 Most Inspiring Women in Indonesia and one of their Asia's 48 Philanthropists, both in 2015. She won the Ernst & Young Social Entrepreneur of the Year in 2011, and the Schwab Foundation's Social Entrepreneur in 2012. She was named as one of the UN Solution Makers in 2017.

Veronica lives in Jakarta with her husband, and they have three children.